IN HIS IMAGE

FINDING TRUTH IN A WORLD OF FALSE IDENTITIES

A memoir

by

Michael A. Cabezas

Dedication

For my mom, who always loves and supports her son, (but knew nothing about the contents of this book beforehand).

For the friends, family, and curious who read this book; may you come to know that God reigns, saves, and satisfies for His glory in Christ Jesus.

Special Thanks

Theodore Brun

Jonathan Wright

Rosa Cabezas Fetterman

Author's Note

Names have been changed to protect the privacy of individuals.

Contents

Foreword

Transformation — that is the best word to describe Michael's life in the past five years since he had a profound encounter with Jesus. His memoir draws the reader into the heart of his desperate journey for significance, acceptance, and love. From the young boy who grew up in Newark, New Jersey, to the "traveling evangelist" who has inspirational conversations with people from various backgrounds and faith traditions, he has been on an accelerated path of studying and applying the Word of God in a way that I have not observed in many other believers.

As the youngest in our family, Michael was perceived as the "quiet one" who kept to himself. It has often been said that the youngest will often struggle to find their voice. Michael has not only found his voice but has also strengthened his resolve to share what God has done in his life through his powerful testimony. It has been an honor to read and proofread his manuscript. It was gripping to discover amazing experiences about my brother's life that stirred up some deep emotions—sadness, regret, shock, and joy. God's provision, grace, and goodness are so evident in each chapter. If God can do what He did for Michael, He can do the same for all others who choose to trust Him with their lives.

Michael is transparent and vulnerable in what he shares while also challenging the reader to go deeper in understanding the truth. His message is simple and yet profound. Only Christ can truly change a person who is fully surrendered to Him. The false identities that this world offers can never compare to the deep, abiding love found in Christ alone. "Therefore, if anyone is in Christ, he is a new creation. The old has passed away; behold, the new has come" (2 Corinthians 5:17).

While working toward his theology degree in Sydney, Australia, Michael completed an internship at a local church and completed his certificate of Christian counselling at the Australian Institute of Family Counselling. Much of his time was spent engaging with youth and preaching the Word of God on Sunday evenings. After graduation Michael immersed himself in the world of apologetics. His thoughtful comments about understanding a person's worldview before engaging the person in a discussion of faith are both admirable and worth paying attention to.

After I finished reading Michael's book, I was left with a longing for more. It has become clearer to me that we all have a story to tell. How much time have we devoted to carefully reflect on how God has been present in our lives? My brother was not a religious person, and his life was centered on what he wanted to do. Now his focus is on engaging people in conversations that are thought-provoking and will hopefully lead them closer to the arms of Jesus. He has described himself as a "gardener" in the kingdom of God. May he faithfully continue planting seeds and cultivating the soil of people's hearts in his journey to glorify God.

Rosa Cabezas Fetterman, Psy.D. Clinical Psychologist
Mount Joy, Pennsylvania

CHAPTER ONE

Seen, Unseen

In the beginning God created… (Genesis 1:1)

All beginnings are good. It's what happens afterwards when things go wrong.

The first memory I have of my beginnings is almost Edenic. I am a little boy sitting on a pew in Saint Francis Xavier Church. There's that thick fragrance of incense in the air typical of any Catholic sanctuary, mingling with the sweet scent of over-waxed pews. It's either the smell of old age — or else holiness, I guess. I never could decide which. It's peaceful. My feet are dangling off the bench, not quite touching the floor.

Ahead of me, beyond the priest, rises a large altarpiece, with pillars of malachite green and a high alcove whose colors shift the light from gold to midnight blue and back again. Christ the Redeemer is looking down at us all from up there. Below him the priest is officiating the Eucharist. His soft voice echoes around the sanctuary: "This is my body, given up for you" (Luke 22:19).

There's a woman in the pew behind me. She's only a young woman, probably in her twenties, but she seems old to me. I know she's there because she's stroking my hair. I wondered why and turn around to look at her. For a long, strange moment she is glowing. I don't know if it's an effect of the sunlight or something else. Her outline almost shimmers, as if a golden haze surrounds her. And she smiles down at me. This golden, loving smile.

I feel seen. And loved.

I am four years old.

Creation

In the beginning, God . . .

I guess the word *creation* didn't mean much to me back then. But at least I had some sense that God had made the world, that He was the creator of all things, though I may not have put it like that, and the world He had placed me in was a city on the outer edge of the urban sprawl of the New York City metropolis — a city called Newark, New Jersey.

Back then it was hardly a paradise. I'm not sure many would describe it as a paradise even today. But I loved it, and it was *my home.*

For those early years my whole existence was contained within a grid of seven or eight blocks. Most of the people who lived among these streets were immigrants of one kind or another, and we were no different.

My parents had come to the United States from Ecuador in 1969. They had come, like so many others, seeking opportunity, hoping for a better life, chasing the promise of the American dream. Both had come from poverty in Ecuador. My mom was especially poor, from a family where her mother literally had no shoes to wear. My dad had grown up in Riobamba, a different region of Ecuador, also poor but eventually worked as an electrician.

The "dream" they were pursuing was exactly that: ephemeral as a vision of the night, as my parents were to discover. The American dream was little more than a marketing slogan to entice immigrants to come to America, conjured up by men like Rockefeller who would never know poverty for themselves. "Come here and you'll prosper" was the lie that so many swallowed. And while my parents never regretted the move they made; my mom especially would tell you how hard it was. The sacrifices made, the costs of what it took to move from Ecuador to the United States — these were a heavy burden to bear. And it may explain some of what happened, particularly to my dad. When you pursue an unrealistic goal or a goal that you think will satisfy and then it doesn't — that can leave you disappointed and angry and full of resentment. As with the Israelites of the Exodus, for many who came to America there was an awful lot of wandering in the desert before they came anywhere near the promised land.

Mom and Dad had come to Newark with a family: my two older sisters, Mary and Rosa; Aunt Jenny; and my grandmother, Mom's mother, also called Rosa. Asking my mom and sisters, I found it hard to pin down exactly what year each of them came over. What is certain is that Mom, Dad, and both of my sisters came first. Grandmother Rosa and Aunt Jenny followed about two years later.

This was already a lot of responsibility for my dad to shoulder as the one man among them. But my parents went on to have two more kids in the United States. They were laying down a marker in their adoptive land, a sign that they were here to stay. The first was my brother, Victor Manuel, known to us as "Manny". And three and a half years later, on May 7, 1979, came me: Michael Anthony Cabezas.

Manny and I were second-generation Americans, raised in 1980s New Jersey and steeped in all that entailed. In those days that meant video games on the PlayStation console, baseball, pizza parties, Michael Jackson, Madonna, Air Jordans, and the rise of baggy jeans. New York was taking off. Wall Street was booming, unemployment was falling, hip-hop was stamping New York City on the cultural map — and if the folk of Newark clung on tightly enough, we just might take off with it too.

But much of that came later.

My earliest memories center on the church of Saint Francis Xavier. I served as an altar boy, following in Manny's footsteps, and as far as I recall that was a good experience for me. It was the first time I discovered how to pull focus on myself. Maybe I needed that, being the youngest — the baby in a family, for which was a lot of competition for attention. But as you'll see, there were other reasons.

In any case, I soon figured out that I could sing. I mean I was no Michael Jackson, but since it was obligatory to participate in church service around once a week as part of our schooling — when two or three classes would traipse down to the sanctuary during school hours and sing hymns

I figured I might as well make the most of it. I made sure I sang out loudly and higher than the other kids. I would catch the glances of my friends, the girls especially, giggling around me. They weren't laughing *at* me but rather *with* me. Their laughter made me feel good. I was halfway between a star and the class clown. And that only encouraged me to sing even harder. My fooling around soon became contagious, and before long several other kids were doing the same.

So, I became the kid who sang loudly in church. And I liked this identity. It was my way of being noticed. And it worked.

The times I served as an altar boy didn't mean I became an especially religious kid. Yet as far as I look back, I can see that I always had a sense that God was around, that He was somehow *there*. That notion seemed completely normal to me. And yet even this simple certainty was something that would slip away from me in time.

You see, no one was mentoring me or leading me in this innate, base-level faith that I had. My family were all Catholics, as most Ecuadorians were, but that hardly made them devout. Faith was there to inform your values, to give you a basic sense of right from wrong. A personal faith in God was not something to take too far. Being over-enthusiastic when it came to God was considered a little weird, to be honest.

There was one exception to this in my family. My sister Rosa, who was fourteen years older than me, had some sort of epiphany when she was twenty. I couldn't tell you exactly how that came about, but I do remember her sitting me down on the couch in our apartment one day — dangling feet again — and trying to convey to me the reality of God and her newfound faith in Jesus as His Son and her Savior. I was barely six years old. Still, I looked up to Rosa. She was my big sister. So, I listened as best I could. But what can a six-year-old kid really grasp of such mysteries?

I do remember Rosa's sincerity, though, very clearly. She had this kind of shimmer of passion rising off her, like heat off a stove. That much stayed with me. And that was really the only time anyone tried to impress on me the beauty and truth about Jesus Christ.

It would take me a lifetime to discover them for myself.

The Garden

Meanwhile, my family had settled into our life in Newark. We were Ecuadorians but our neighborhood at that time was predominantly Italian. We lived in an apartment in a multifamily housing tract on 7th Street, on the block between 2nd and 3rd Avenues. Our apartment was decorated "old school." This was the mid-1980s, but our place was still done up in 1970s style. The furniture, the wallpaper, the fittings — everything in yellows, oranges, and greens, all color schemes which, looking back, one wonders how on earth anyone thought were a good idea. But that was the backdrop to my early life. Mom was especially big on green. And the apartment didn't change much in the twenty years we lived there.

Decor aside, our home was a lively place, full of people. My parents threw a lot of parties at that time. Pretty much every weekend, people would start arriving in the evening and would just keep on coming, drinking and dancing through the night — to cumbia, always cumbia, it seemed, and sometimes merengue. I can still feel the beat of all that old-school Spanish music pulsing through my memories.

Singers like Julio Iglesias and José Feliciano. As I said, we lived among a lot of Italians, but most of my parents' friends were Latinos (folk from Latin America), and naturally they were determined to keep their culture, especially its music, alive and well.

You can read about how the different ethnic communities in Newark became more integrated later on. Latinos — mostly from Puerto Rico, Mexico, Peru, and the Dominican Republic — and then various African cultures started mixing. It was out of this cultural cross-pollination, if you can call it that, that hip-hop emerged, just at the moment, MTV was finding its feet, which did a lot to spread it to a global audience. We didn't realize it at the time, but that little area of the New York metropolis would become impactful on music across the world, both for good and bad reasons.

Still, back in those days, for us anyway, it was all cumbia, merengue, and salsa.

My parents were extroverts. They liked company. And I was the little kid in the household, the baby of the party, surrounded by a lot of adults towering over me, drinking probably more than they should at the end of a long week. My memories of those parties are a swirl of jarring laughter, grinning faces, bright makeup, and strong perfume; the clink of beer bottles, swaying hips, and the pulse of "our" music under it all. My sister says that later in the evenings there would often be arguments and even fights spilling out onto the street. But I don't remember that. Those parties felt like good times.

It's true, there was already a lot of alcohol in our lives. Probably that was an extension of my dad and the culture in general. As you'll see, alcohol was a growing presence in his life.

His name was Victor.

For as long as I knew him, he worked down at the waterfront as a longshoreman. Newark, pronounced more like *No'ark* in one long, drawled syllable, had for a long time been an integral part of the Port of New York and New Jersey. Although by the 1970s the era of the classic longshoreman — at least as it's depicted in the Brando movie *On the Waterfront* – had faded away. In its place new shipping container terminals had been built, supported by new transportation systems that would service all the shipping trade flowing in and out of the country. This was the beating industrial and economic heart of Newark, and Dad was right in the middle of it.

As a longshoreman, he worked to the bone, especially as an immigrant. He was responsible for maintaining and fixing a lot of heavy plant machinery in and around the docks. That meant cranes, trucks, and forklifts. It also meant preparing outgoing cargoes for loading, plus unloading the cargoes coming in. It was a lot of grease and dirt and sweat and oil, breaking his knuckles trying to undo nuts that were frozen solid. It was all outdoor work — steam and swelter in the summer, ice and snow and bitter winds that cut right through you in the winter.

The winters were long in New Jersey. The work was heavy. The hours were long, too. Besides all this, as an Ecuadorian, Dad was an outsider. He was subjected to some pretty bad discrimination and verbal abuse over the years, especially from the Italians, who saw themselves as having been there first. To them, he was nothing but a "spic" (a derogatory term for Hispanics, which itself isn't much better). The way they saw it, he was beneath them and always would be.

All of this took its physical toll on my father. He had two knee operations that I remember. But the mental and emotional toll was just as high. Decades of bullying changes a man. There was a lot of anger there. And I guess he didn't know where to put it.

After work he wouldn't come home right away. Instead, he used to go to a local Portuguese bar — the Ponderosa or Iberia — in the Ironbound district of East Newark to drink and unwind with his buddies. Probably at first it was for a beer, maybe two. But as time went on, he would stay out longer, drink more, until eventually it became normal for him to get home when I was supposed to be getting ready for bed, often even later. Sometimes he would bring me a bar of chocolate when he came back late, at least enough times that even when he didn't, I would force myself to lie awake in my bed, waiting for the sound of the door latch — just in case I got lucky.

These days as a man looking back, I find it easier to recognize the heavy pall of frustration that must have settled over him: his disappointment at the broken American dream, the weariness and monotony of his job, the daily abuse and humiliation at the hands of his coworkers, the quiet rage burning like a furnace in his belly.

But as a kid I couldn't understand what he was going through.

I just got the sense of seeing him less and less, knowing him less and less — and he not knowing much of me either, or wanting to. For me he became a sort of ghost in the home. There but not really there. I think I feared him more than anything else. And yet I still yearned for his love.

My name is Michael, but I never once recall my Dad using it, except perhaps when he was mad. Usually, he just called me *hijo*.

Son.

Unseen

Mostly then, my brother and I were raised among women, although Manny probably had more time among men than I did, since I was the baby of the family. And Manny was at least my dad's elder son.

Mom was a schoolteacher and would work every day till about 3 p.m. My two sisters were older, though I don't remember them being at home that much because they were at college at the time. Aunt Jenny lived in the basement apartment of our building with Grandma Rosa. I spent a lot of time down there, or else being closely monitored on the second floor, being minded by my Abuelita (grandmother) when my parents were out.

Even so, Mom was the glue among all of us. She was very warm, very forgiving, with a heart of gold (She had to be, as Dad became increasingly angry and irritable with the effects of his alcoholism). And she was always very clear about right from wrong. Her moral values were essentially conservative, instilled in her by her Catholic faith, such as it was. Being so close to her and the other women in our family made me more sensitive, I guess — softer, more emotional. And when my brother went on to high school ahead of me, any male influence in my young life was limited, although my father's absence had its own effect.

Absence *is* influence, if you like.

I'm sure that lack of attention from my father created a hunger for it, a hunger I had to satisfy in other ways. But I'll talk about that more in the next chapter.

There was only one time I can recall when, for once, I did feel seen by him.

I was playing little league baseball, and since he was home at five o'clock and practice started at six, Mom told him that he should take me. He agreed and I remember riding along beside him in the car feeling excitement. The thought in my head was *He's actually going to watch me play.* Coach put me in the shortstop position that day. As I waited for the next pitch, I could glance behind me and see my dad sitting up in the stands, watching me. *That's my Dad. There he is.* It made me feel like the other kids for once, whose fathers were often there. I must have been grinning all the way through that game. It was a moment I'll never forget.

But then the game ended, and we got in the car and drove home. I waited and waited for him to say something. Anything. But we just sat in silence all the way. No "Good job, son." No "Well played today, son." Any word of affirmation would have been as precious as gold to me. But instead, silence. He was present but *not* present. I have no idea what he was thinking about all the way home.

Maybe he didn't know what to say. He just didn't have it in him.

He never came to watch me again.

The Serpent

At the time the place we lived in was a relatively nice urban neighborhood. Still working class, but not yet gone into the decline that it did in more recent years.

It was only three blocks to my Catholic school and a few blocks in another direction to the baseball park where Manny and I spent an ever-increasing amount of our time. Then there was the Finish Line Pizzeria on the corner of 3rd and 8th. Everyone knew it was mafia-owned, but it was the only joint for us kids to eat and hang out at, so that's where we would go.

To be honest, I have a lot of fond memories of that place and that time. We could come and go without our parents as we pleased, or in my case, if I was with my brother. We would play wiffle ball or soccer in front of our house. Sometimes we would just roam around the neighborhood with a group of friends, all within a ten-minute walk of home.

Eventually the vibe would change with the crackdowns on the mafia (in our case, the Gambino family) in the late 80s and 90s, and then with different ethnic groups moving into the area, Puerto Ricans and African Americans mostly. The streets became edgier, more ghetto, probably less safe for young kids roaming around. The Italians moved out. And it seemed from one day to the next the neighborhood was completely different.

As a kid I was never aware of whatever crime was happening around me. My parents somehow sheltered me from all of that. If I went out, I had to tell them where I was going. I couldn't just sneak out or else I could expect Dad's leather belt to say "Hi" to my rear end when I returned. So, they — mainly Mom, in fact — kept a good eye on me while still allowing me a little freedom.

Part of that freedom meant that after my brother moved up to high school, I would walk to and from school alone. It wasn't far to Saint Francis Xavier School, only three blocks straight up 7th Street, as I said. But even that was long enough for "incidents" to occur.

One of them, I think, was significant. I still remember it very clearly, it being really one encounter in three parts.

I was seven years old. I was on my own and nearly at school, only a block away, head down, minding my own business, as Mom had told me to do.

Up ahead a boy was sitting on his porch watching me approach. As I drew closer, I noticed a sort of dark look on his face. He reminded me of one of those stone gargoyles stuck on the side of mediaeval cathedrals that you sometimes see in books. A sort of malevolent glint could be seen in his eye. Suddenly he got up and stepped out on the sidewalk in front of me. He must have been about nine years old. I didn't recognize him from my school and figured he must have been a kid from the public school right across the street from St. Francis Xavier. There was always animosity between the kids from each school, but I had never experienced it in person until now.

He squared up to me, toe to toe. He was a good few inches taller than me. "Hey" was all he said, blocking my path.

In this moment I felt completely helpless. Mom, Dad, my brother — none of them were there. I was on my own, with no clue as to whether this kid wanted to fight me or what.

Without warning, he stepped forward and shoved me hard. I went flying backward and hit the pavement, cracking the back of my head on the concrete. I looked up at him, pain ringing through my skull, a helpless look on my face that said, *Why are you doing this to me?*

"You're not going to school right now," he snarled.

A faint "What?" was all I could manage in reply as I tried to stand. I was sure he was about to swing at me, but his fist stayed low. Instead, I got to my feet and fled.

I ran and ran until a couple of minutes later I arrived breathlessly at the school gate.

The entire remainder of the day in class I couldn't stop thinking about what had happened. I was so confused. Why would someone do that to me? Who *was* that kid? Did he know me? What had I ever done to him? Why did he want to hurt me? Humiliate me?

I had no answers.

I never spoke to anyone about that incident. I carried it all inside—the fear I had felt, the knowledge that I hadn't fought back, that I had barely been able to voice an objection.

It was only shortly afterwards that I had my second encounter with this boy.

I was leaving school after class. I was not far out of the school gate when I saw him lurking a little way down the street. I angled away from him and began running, not a full sprint but kind of jogging away from him — except that he had already seen me and moved to cut me off.

"Where d'you think you're going?" he said.

Now I broke into a sprint, astonished because no one had ever talked to me like that. His legs were longer than mine and he soon caught up with me and cornered me. This time he put up his dukes. He wanted to fight. All I could do was to cower away from him. I had no clue how to defend myself. A thought flashed through my head: *I should call the police.* But how? Instead, I fled again, this time in the opposite direction.

It was already getting dark, so I ran back toward the school with him hot on my tail. I saw the rectory and a figure inside, someone I recognized, a friend of my brother's named Ariel. I could see him through the window. He was working, just getting off the phone.

If I can just get him to notice me . . . I'll be saved.

But then the other kid was there.

"You're not going to run this time. Come on and fight me." I knew I should stand up to him. I didn't want to be a coward. But I just couldn't. Instead, I darted around to the rectory door and leaned on the bell as if it would open the gates of heaven.

The door swung open, and Ariel filled the frame. "Mikey? Is that you? What's going on? What're you doing here?"

I rushed past him into the hallway. "I'm all right. I'm all right," I panted. "I just . . . I just need to get home."

"Sure, you do, kid. But isn't home the other way?"

I can't remember what excuses I made or what explanation I gave him. But I know I didn't tell the truth, didn't reach for help when it was right there in front of me.

I was ashamed, ashamed that I knew for sure now that I was indeed, a coward — and feared that I always would be.

You may think I'm making too much of this, but I remember the profound effect it had on me — that feeling of cowardice and fear that came into me then, like an injection into my veins, flowing right through my body, growing into a flood of fear that would carry me through that time and into my teenage years. I didn't have the fortitude to stand up for myself. That was the ugly truth, I concluded. But neither did I have the courage to ask someone for help. Dad wasn't there — to stand up for me or to teach me how to stand up for myself. He was working too hard, drinking too hard. He had always been a great family provider — we certainly had a better life because of his strong work ethic. He drove himself as hard as any man reasonably could. He's also the reason my brother and I got to go to Catholic primary school and then high school. However, the relentlessness of his job meant he drank to numb the pain. That came with a price for all of us — and the price I paid was his ignoring me.

You might think that at that tender age I could find a way to connect with him. I wanted to. Boy, I wanted to. I remember him sitting at our faded kitchen table, yellow paint peeling off its surface, a can of Budweiser nestled behind the wall of his knuckles. I wanted to reach out and touch his hand. But I couldn't. Just couldn't reach him. He was watching TV on a tiny set we had mounted on the kitchen table. Even when I did summon the courage to touch his arm, he would come to himself as if waking out of a trance, then just continue ignoring me or telling me to go play, all without taking his eyes from the screen. Probably a soccer game was on or maybe *The Benny Hill Show,* which was his favorite.

Some days he would be watching *The Twilight Zone*. He was always watching those shows, which hardly made appropriate viewing for a kid. One of them featured an overweight British comedian who was forever being chased by girls in bikinis on fast forward. The other show consisted of weird stories of the spooky and paranormal. If I could have, I would have sneaked up alongside him and just sat there in the room with him, watching the program but understanding very little. These shows seemed to be his way to "not think," to switch off, lost in a kind of twilight zone himself — there but not really there.

I seemed to be just as transparent to him, a ghost haunting his elbow. I was just *hijo* — son. One of two. I didn't even merit the specificity of my name.

The third time I ran into the bully again was when I was walking to school. I hadn't seen him in a while. But that morning there he was. My first instinct was to cross the road, to walk by on the other side, and I turned to do so. But there was so much traffic, cars zooming past every few seconds, that I just kept going on the same side.

Fear filled my limbs like liquid metal, and I continued walking, making them feel heavy. Our eyes meet. But this time he didn't move from his perch. He just sat there, watching me. As I passed, he stood up, and I was sure he was going to come down, at least say something. But instead, he just stood there, staring at me.

Please don't do anything, I was thinking. Please, please just stay where you are.

That look in his eye. He had his mark on me. *I see you.*

I felt seen, only this time not by something good — by a snake in the grass, a serpent in the garden.

I see you, too, the serpent said.

CHAPTER TWO

Hide & Seek

It is a joy to be hidden and a disaster not to be found.
- D.W. Winnicott

Maybe it was the lack of attention from my father. Maybe I'm just a product of my environment. But I've always had a thirst to be noticed, as if I had some deficit to make up.

I learned at an early age that singing was one way to get people to notice me. The other was baseball.

Baseball became a focal point from early on. First my brother, Manny, discovered he had a talent for it, and a few years after him, so did I. Baseball became my first love, you could say, and a huge part of our world at the time. The only team anyone in our neighborhood could ever dream of supporting was the New York Yankees, although if you looked hard enough you might find the occasional Mets fan. The Yankees were riding high all through the mid-1980s even though despite long winning streaks and having the best record of any team in the major leagues, they still never managed to take the World Series and made the playoffs only twice. That was in 1980 and 1981, when I was barely out of diapers. Still, the near misses didn't stop people hoping with each new season that "This will be the year."

For our Ecuadorian family, the soccer World Cup was just as popular. But personally, I didn't get it. I mean, sometimes I would watch it with them. But their enthusiasm for "the beautiful game" was definitely *their* thing, something they had brought over with them from Ecuador. The excitement of watching those games created some fond memories, but I always had a sense that I was just different from the other members of my family, as if I belonged somewhere else — or rather *to* someone else.

I came across a similar feeling to this when I first read about Abraham, the Old Testament patriarch. He felt like a stranger in his own land, untethered, looking forward to "the city that has foundations, whose designer and builder is God" (Hebrews 11:10). That very well describes how I sometimes felt. Of course, I never would have formed a thought in my head in that language, but looking back, I can see traces of that sense of dislocation, as if my true home, my true belonging, were elsewhere.

But how could that be?

In any case, you would be hard-pressed to find anyone who is a genuine fan of both soccer *and* baseball. There was never any question about where my loyalties lay.

Afterall, we had a good team to look up to in the Yankees or else I had discovered I could really play; I became obsessed with baseball from the age of six and eventually started collecting baseball cards. I lived and breathed it, alongside Manny, whom I also looked up to a lot. Both of us proved to be pretty good players, too.

More good memories come from little league, when I was playing in Newark Stadium for Tony D Electric, then later when I was playing high school ball for the Golden Griffins, though that may be because in little league I hadn't hit puberty yet — which, as you'll see, created its own problems.

Over the span of years Manny and I won a ton of trophies, many of which are still sitting on the shelf in Mom's home today. I loved the game for itself, sure. But I also enjoyed the affirmation it gave me. Who wouldn't? Winning at baseball became a central part of my identity — being good at something. People noticed. I liked that. I needed that.

On the other hand, when it came to academics I was *unlike* my brother. Manny was a straight-A student. I was more like a decent C student. I remember looking at his report card and seeing all As, then looking at mine and thinking, *I want what he's got.* For this reason and many others, I admired my big brother. He was a better athlete than me, popular, and very charismatic. And at the same time, he was always very encouraging to me, a great role model for a little Ecuadorian kid growing up in Jersey.

But however much I would have loved to emulate him, it was clear that I was never going to impress anyone in the classroom — especially and increasingly important, the girls except by making them laugh, which really meant fooling around.

It was all harmless stuff, although our teacher, Miss LaGuardia, may not have agreed. No doubt she failed to appreciate most of the things we would put in her morning coffee. But by my reckoning, I paid my dues with the many detentions I had to sit through. Besides, the payoff was worth it. The girls (and boys) in our class would laugh. That was enough for me — even though every time I got detention, I was terrified of what would happen when I got home. Fortunately, it was usually Mom who took the call from the principal's office, and she rarely told Dad that I had been in trouble.

That didn't mean she *never* told him I had been bad.

There was one incident at home when I was nine or ten. I was playing outside with Manny and one of his friends in the backyard. I can't remember the exact provocation; probably I was being a complete brat. My brother was often having to tell me to shut up because I was so spoiled (and it showed when I spoke to our neighborhood friends). But whatever it was, suddenly I was mouthing off at Manny with some pretty foul language, telling him exactly what I thought of him. Unfortunately for me, Mom was hanging laundry on the second floor with the window wide open and she heard me. I believe she was shocked that I knew that kind of language already, and boy, was I in for it!

She yelled at me to get myself upstairs. And just the minute or two it took me to traipse, lead-footed, up the stairs, desperately trying to muster the courage to face her, was punishment enough. When I got up there, I discovered my next ordeal was to chew on a bar of soap for half an hour. And she was so mad she also said she would tell Dad when he got home. Sure enough, I was in bed when I heard him get in, cowering under my covers. I listened to the voices down the hall, the sudden escalation in volume and temper, the clomp-clomp of his boots down the corridor and the door bursting open. And there was the belt.

I think anyone with a South American upbringing of a certain age can probably relate. The belt was half an inch thick of solid brown leather. And man, that thing hurt! When I say we would get whipping, I mean a whipping. If we knew it was coming, Manny and I would deaden the pain by stuffing towels down our pants. But usually, it was all done on the spur of the moment and over in seconds, while tempers were high — which somehow feels better than a cold, calculated punishment ritual. It was all part of the chaos of a Latino family (even if knowing that didn't help my rear end any).

The Fall

Whenever Mom wasn't around, busy with work or something else, we were left with Grandma Rosa (whom we called "Abuelita") in the basement apartment. Of the two of us boys, Manny was always my Abuelita's favorite. She thought I was basically a mama's boy, over-spoiled and in need of toughening up. To be fair to her, I was mischievous when I was put under her care. It wasn't unknown for her to launch a *chancla* (house slipper) at my head when I had been misbehaving. Fortunately, her aim wasn't as sharp as her tongue.

There was one summer — I was about nine years old — when my junior high school was already out about a week before Manny's high school broke for summer recess. My sisters were adults by then and were no longer at home all that much. So, I would spend days and days under the watchful eye of Abuelita Rosa. She would make me eat her homemade soup. I never liked it, maybe because I was always being force-fed it (Of course, ever since her passing from dementia, I now miss her soup terribly, along with the good old times). In fact, I didn't eat much as a child in general. I recall my mouth often being forced open to eat during dinner and the echoes of my family, especially my Abuelita, telling me to "just eat!" These somewhat traumatic moments were no more fun for her than they were for me. I was always asking her when Mom was coming home, telling her, "You can't tell me what to do!"

I probably deserved a lot of the grief I got from her.

One afternoon I had invited a friend to come outside and play ball in the backyard. Except we had no ball. So, I had the bright idea that we could find one in the garage at the back of the property, even though I was forbidden to go in there unsupervised. Dad used to keep a car in there and for a while a motorbike too. But mostly it was crammed with all kinds of junk, strewn with old boxes and dirty dust sheets. Technically the roller door was locked, but it was still possible to crawl under the bottom if we both hefted it up and wedged it open with a milk-crate.

I snuck underneath, no idea of what was waiting there for me in the dark.

Eventually, I found a light switch, adrenaline already buzzing in my veins. If my Abuelita found me in there, I could expect the right hand to go up and . . . *wallop!* But worse, Dad might find out I was rummaging through his stuff, and that would mean the belt.

I started going through boxes, exploring the uncharted territory of what a man like my father might collect over the course of a lifetime. I told myself I was looking for a ball, but really, I was just poking my beak into everything. I wasn't alone in there often, so I was determined to make the most of it now. There were a lot of old tools and other stuff that I probably shouldn't be alone with — a big sledgehammer, a wood saw, other hammers, a staple gun—all of it tempting for a nine-year-old boy. Then some old luggage under layers of dust, a couple of ten-speed bikes with rusted tires, and boxes stacked one on top of the other in the far right of the garage, which for some reason creeped me out. They seemed the perfect hiding place for an oversized rat, or even a monster.

Just then my buddy called through the gap that he was taking off.

"No, wait a sec — I'm nearly done!"

"I'm not standing out here like a doofus, Mikey. We're gonna get caught. You can look out for yourself." With that, off he went. I let him go, too intent now on what I was doing.

Then I opened a box and there it was — a stack of magazines. They looked old and worn, although they hadn't completely lost the gloss off their covers. Almond-eyed girls with long, dark hair gazed up at me with smiles that seemed half-bored, half-inviting. I couldn't have known at once what I was looking at, that I had stumbled across my old man's stash of porn.

I suppose most people, young boys especially, have had this moment of discovery, like the breaking of a seal, a moment never to be undone. These days it's far too easy. It's all there at the click of a computer mouse.

Opening those thumbed pages, my eyes stretched wide in astonishment, a kind of electric current passing into my fingers from the paper, racing up my arms and through my body. At first, I didn't know what I was looking at. I had the impression of skin, flesh . . . *meat.* And the rush of a sort of spirit came over me. I was nine years old. What did I know about the power of lust? Yet suddenly this feeling was pouring over me like a cataract of scalding water. And that was it. That was my innocence being burned right off me. I could never unsee what I had seen.

"Michael, are you in there?" Abuelita Rosa's voice came sharp and shrill, slipping in like my conscience under the roller door.

I have no idea how many pages I had leafed through by then. I couldn't have been there for very long, but I remember thinking, *I'm so gonna get my butt whipped for this!*

I shoved everything back as fast as I could and returned the box to where I had found it before emerging outside with a very guilty look on my face. Abuelita was not impressed, although she never found out the true cause of my embarrassment. Her right arm came up, but I was quicker, scampering round her and fleeing back into the house. I got an ear-full off her later, but that time I managed to avoid the *chancla.*

Once I got over the shock of what I had seen, as I said, it was as if a seal had been broken. Shock gave way to curiosity. I returned to the garage again the very next day. And then again, and again. Sometimes alone, sometimes I'd bring a buddy along to paw over the magazines with me. It felt good to have an accomplice. But it also felt good to get kudos from my buddies, to have something we knew was illicit to share with my friends.

Of course, I had no clue of the damage that it was doing to my perception of sex and of women in general. Sound familiar? Nine years old is *way* too young to be exposed to all that stuff, especially when those pornographic images were really all I had to go on as I grew into adolescence.

Those magazines were the main source of instruction when it came to learning what sex was all about. Of course, everything in their pages is an utter delusion, but I never knew that. And Dad was never going to tell me anything about women. He never even taught me how to stand up for myself.

There was no way he was ever going to explain the intricacies (or intimacies) of sex to either of his sons. As for Mom, it wasn't her place. Anyway, I was too shy to bring up anything like that with her during the teenage years that followed. So, I was left with *Hustler* and *Playboy* magazines as my guides, and later the distorted perceptions and misadventures of my teenage peers. It's only these many years later that I can look back and see how damaging this early exposure to porn was to my understanding of what healthy sexual relations with a woman could and should be.

And yet, innocent as I was at that time, it wasn't as if I was wholly unaccountable. I still knew right and wrong. I knew I shouldn't have been in that garage. I knew I shouldn't have been looking through that stuff. I was going to church every Sunday. I had a vague sense that God was real and that He was there. I knew this stuff wasn't what He wanted for me. On the other hand, there was no compelling reason to obey my conscience, or at least no reason compelling enough to *make* me obey my conscience. Whatever faith I had, it rarely demanded of me any kind of sacrifice, especially when there were stronger forces pulling me away from what I knew to be right and good.

Sometimes the reckoning of that takes a long time coming.

But one day it would.

When I recall this episode, it brings to my mind the story of that first loss of innocence in the Garden of Eden. We call it "the fall." But what was that? Adam and Eve falling for the temptation to know more than they needed to know, more than God wanted them to know. Why? Because they heeded the voice of the snake in the grass over the quiet but clear instruction of their own consciences. And what was the result? They hid. They felt shame.

The different influences I've described so far were drawing together, patterns of personality that would determine the path that I was going to walk in the next passage of years to come, away from the God who had made himself present to me — and toward something else. Something . . .

Well, you'll see.

But already this unlooked-for knowledge, this loss of innocence had covered me in a kind of shame. That shame led to a further kind of hiding. Whatever confidence I had up until then depended on the attention and good opinion of others. In many ways I was Mr. Popular. But all that affirmation was from the outside coming in — while inside me there was no strong answer to that essential question *Who am I?*

And such stirrings of an answer to that question that there gave me no assurance whatsoever. I was the boy who ran away. I was a coward. I knew that if there was a dominating force, good or bad, pressing me one way over another, I would surrender to it. That was easier than taking a stand.

This was a pattern I would follow for a long, long time.

Into Hiding

Growing into my teenage years, the "hiding" became more pronounced. That's normal for a teenage boy, I guess, especially when there's a lot of confusion on the inside and not a lot of guidance on the outside. Who was I supposed to be? What was I supposed to do? Not knowing which direction I was supposed to take, I shrank from taking any direction at all.

I still had my baseball and my video games. Both served to escape the reality in which I found myself. The video gaming world became my "go-to" distraction. It helped because it numbed my intellectual capacity to think. *Mario Brothers* and *Sonic the Hedgehog* were the popular games at this time. My brother and I would sit for hours playing them. There were others we played, like *Contra, MLB, FIFA,* and *NFL.* But when the games would "freeze up" and stop functioning, as they often did back then, I would be looking for another distraction.

The false confidence I had gotten from fooling around in class took a big knock when I went through puberty and suffered from a severe form of cystic acne that showed up all over my face. As a skin condition, it was painful and irritable enough. But perhaps more significantly, it robbed me of the small measure of confidence I had enjoyed with the girls of my age. Having been seen as attractive before, I now thought I was ugly. Life was over for me — at least that's how it felt.

Probably that sounds stupid and superficial. But every teenage boy knows how fragile self-esteem can be at that age and how easily it can be shattered. Looking at my face in the mirror only made me want to hide it. That feeling was real. And then I got braces on my teeth, which made it even worse.

As the desire to hide away grew, I got more into video games. I spent hours in my room playing *Madden NFL* and survival horror games like *Resident Evil.* By now Victor had left high school. I rarely saw him after that. He was in college, Rutgers University, focusing on getting on with his life. I don't blame him. He didn't know how empty and lonely I felt. No one did. So being the last chick to fly the nest, I was left to my own devices, my own self-gratification, probably the last thing I needed.

Meanwhile there were more arguments at home about Dad's drinking — even some physical abuse, of which I became more aware as I grew older, pushing and shoving, breaking stuff around the house. Despite it all, Mom was always ready to forgive him. I don't know how she did it, to be honest. She was like some kind of saint for many, many years. I believe it's only because of her that we siblings all made it through relatively unscathed. But maybe that's an illusion too. Perhaps we all bear the scars in different ways. I'm sure my sisters, for example, would tell a different story.

Certainly, as the baby of the family, I had been shielded from a lot of this for a long time. But once I reached fourteen or fifteen, it was no longer possible to hide it from me.

The slipper. The *chancla.* Yeah, the slipper. And the belt. We saw a lot of that when we misbehaved.

I was the lucky one, though. If Dad's rage was a waterfall, it had already gone down several sets of rapids before it got to my level, which sapped a lot of its intensity. Mom and my older siblings bore the worst of it. I only got the scraps of his rage — but also the scraps of his attention, the scraps of *him*.

I'm able to see this now only because I better understand the boy I was then, how I had a very specific personality that needed attention in general, maybe more so than other kids, needed the attention of a father, needed not to be ignored. So now, because of who I am, I can see that his ignoring me *was* a kind of abuse.

Of course, I couldn't have understood this at the time. Nor did I know that my father had grown up with his own set of problems. Like me, he didn't have the fatherly attention he needed either. Beyond that, it's hard to fathom the family history. But I would be willing to bet that this whole "absentee father" thing goes back generations, reliably passed on father-to-son like a cherished heirloom. I can only pray that I'm able to break the chain when the time comes.

Through most of this I was simply observing, and little more, all the time pulling away from him, pulling away from my environment. My focus outside of the house was baseball and girls — until the acne, which gave me further reason to pull back. Schoolwork came in a distant third if it was lucky. Gaming increased.

And then around the age of eighteen — in fact around the time that I stopped playing baseball—I, too, started drinking, as you'll see.

It wasn't even the usual teenage peer pressure sort of drinking either. You know the kind — youths experimenting with alcohol to puff themselves up, to "feel like a man." Nah. Right from the start I was drinking to forget, to numb myself. That was all I had ever seen modeled to me, both out there in our culture — the movies we watched, the music we listened to — and also closer to home. I drank to turn away from reality, not because reality was intrinsically so unlivable for me, but rather because I didn't know how to engage with it, to get on in it. The truth was that I didn't *want* to meet the world head-on as it was.

So, I hid.

Looking back, I think I was suffering from a mild form of depression. I would spend hours on the computer at home looking for treatments for my acne. It became an obsession, a kind of externalization of my other problems. In looking for a solution to my acne, I was seeking a solution to everything that felt wrong inside of me. It was possible to do this in the confines of my room even then, in the mid-1990s. It's even easier to slip into that pattern these days. There are so many more rabbit holes to fall down on the Internet with endless YouTube channels and all the other social media and streaming platforms.

Young people are particularly susceptible to that. I'm not even talking about the classic conspiracy theory rabbit holes as such, religious cults, or any of the other more obvious things that can colonize the mind. I'm talking more about the idea that, because of some other pain in a young person's life, he or she becomes fixated on a particular thing — something that becomes more than a passion and grows into an obsession, something that starts consuming all the young person's time and energy and headspace when really what is needed is to reach outward, to talk to someone else about how he or she is feeling, to connect with someone who cares about him or her, however hard it may be to take that step.

Again, back to the garden . . .

When Adam and Eve were hiding, knowing they had done wrong, God walked in the garden and called to them. It was only when they were willing to reveal themselves and speak to Him that God could begin to address the hurt they were feeling, to ease their guilt and their shame. But it's painful to reach out into the light when every fiber in you wants to hide in the dark.

Reality can be hard. But I discovered that deferring engagement with it only makes it much harder.

It doesn't matter whether you're hiding on YouTube channels, in the artificial realities of video gaming, or cocooning yourself in a false identity that you've conjured up out of thin air — merely to escape . . . *yourself.* The rubber always hits the road eventually. Reality always kicks back. And if you aren't going to lose too much skin when that happens, it's better to engage with reality sooner rather than later.

I can see that now.

But back then, how could I?

Even so, my voluntary isolation was not absolute. At the beginning of my teenage years — my first year of high school to be exact — I made a friend who would become my partner in crime, so to speak. His name was Saul.

Up until then I had enjoyed a scattering of friendships through primary school and on into high school. But that changed quite quickly. For reasons I've tried to explain, I soon withdrew from more or less all of them.

Only this friend, Saul, stuck with me through that time.

Tunneling

To this day, Saul remains one of my good friends. It's been decades now. The first time I met him, I was walking into the cafeteria of Queen of Peace High School. Because Dad would drop me off on his way to work, I was one of only three students to get in that early in the morning. I hated it, to be honest, not being much of a morning person.

That day Saul was sitting at a table, dreads hanging down, reading the *Daily News* sports section. I went over, sat next to him, and asked him what was going on.

I soon discovered that he was a die-hard Mets and Knicks fan, the perfect foil for a Yankee and Chicago Bulls fan like me. We always had a lot to talk about.

But aside from sports chat, it was really gaming that brought us together. There was also a sensitivity in him that we both had in common. He had gone through something in his younger days — I'm not sure exactly what — but things like that were never discussed. Maybe this is what enabled us to feed off each other's energy. We did the same things. We played the same video games.

Our friendship was also based on a lot of the things we *didn't* do together. We *didn't* go out to parties like the other kids of our age. We *didn't* socialize the way the rest of them would. We were different from our peers — but really not in a way that's anything to boast about. We missed out on a lot of things, which we made up for later when we turned seventeen, things we thought were too obvious. Instead, we immersed ourselves in our video games, and Saturday nights we would watch UFC (Ultimate Fight Championship) on Pay-per-View TV.

That was what we did. That was who we were.

That's what we told ourselves, anyway. No doubt we didn't want to admit to ourselves that all we were doing was running away from a reality we didn't know how to handle.

Eventually we emerged from our reclusive adolescence together when we were eighteen. I knew some other kids at school who had gotten fake IDs. Manny had mentioned it to me once how important it was to get one and I never forgot it. So, with his help I used his information — birth certificate, Social Security number, and so on — and suggested that Saul do the same. He had an older brother too. In the state of New Jersey, you had to be twenty-one to get into most bars and clubs, or to buy liquor at all. Our fake IDs were our tickets to adulthood. So we figured.

A lot of cultures recognize the importance of certain rites of passage that a boy must go through to become a man. Often, it's the father who must bring his son to this bridge from boyhood to manhood, then lead him across it. Of course, Dad hadn't done that for me; he didn't know how. So, instead of a bridge to manhood, Saul and I had tunneled our way through the darkness and out the other side, emerging into the bright lights of adult life, blinking like moles.

There's something ironic in the fact that these precious IDs these tickets into this new and hazardous world — were fake.

They were as fake as the identities we had been creating for ourselves.

CHAPTER THREE

Leaving the Garden

The way to love anything is to realize that it may be lost.
- G.K. Chesterton

I was now entering a new world.

If my fake ID was the passport, then Sound Garden was the port of entry.

Sound Garden was a nightclub in Lodi, New Jersey, where a lot of young people from the surrounding towns would go. It had one of those long-arched awnings out front to add a bit of class, as if you were some movie star, arriving for a premier. On Friday nights they had live bands; Saturday it was dance music. It was a pretty generic place, I guess, with the same house music that was being played all over Jersey at the time; the same late-90s club vibe, high-back booths, and vinyl leather seats; the same outfits, the same drinks; tequila shots, Jäger bombs — that sort of thing.

But to an eighteen-year-old boy it had all the allure of paradise. Right from the start, I felt that draw. Mostly it was the magnetic force of a place where I could meet women.

That was the most obvious attraction for me. But there were other undertows, too. It was like entering a sensory garden of sights and smells and, yeah, sounds too. Flashes of color, curvaceous silhouettes moving in time with the music, my head buzzing with alcohol, feeling that weird blend of confidence and insecurity that every young man feels when he enters a place like that: a young lion making his first solo foray into the jungle.

You had to be eighteen to get into a place like that, twenty-one to drink. With my fake ID, that wasn't a problem. And once I had tasted the scene, I kept coming back for more. It was compelling, exciting, even if something in me, some flicker of conscience, knew that I was diving into a world that would take me away from God.

Not that I identified that feeling as "God" explicitly in my mind. It was more a sense of "goodness" or what was "right." Looking back, really, I see that they amount to the same thing: I had a sense that I was getting into things that I shouldn't be. After all, just being there, I was breaking the law, even though everybody else was doing it, too. But worse, I was ignoring that quiet wooing voice of conscience — riding roughshod right over it, in fact. These days I might call it rebellion against God's gentle grace to keep me from bad things. But back then — hey, I was young and stupid, and it was justified by cultural norms. So, I went ahead with it.

The more I went to the bars and the clubs, the more that little flame of conscience was quenched; the more I was drowning out that small voice of prompting with the next Jager shot.

These days when I read in the Bible the story of the Israelites being led out of Egypt, rescued from a lifetime of slavery and humiliation, it seems almost unbelievable that those same individuals should so quickly fall away from their faith of following the true God, even after witnessing a miracle as epic as the parting of the Red Sea. They knew. They had seen with their own eyes. And yet within days and weeks they were harking back to their time in Egypt. Because the present way through the desert was hard, many of them preferred the idea of returning to slavery. And before long, as stated in the book of Exodus, most of them were fallen away, drunk and cavorting like fools, worshiping a golden calf, an idol they had seen made with human hands.

Why?

One reason I can think of — peer pressure. Folks just went along with the crowd. It was easier to do than simply to think for themselves, to make a decision they knew to be good but would put them in the minority.

Seeing things that way, I can hardly judge them. I was doing exactly the same thing, myself.

Most of us have.

Of course, from a certain viewpoint, all we were doing was completely normal. Saul and I were exploring, expanding our world, merely doing what we figured adults were supposed to do: go to clubs, check out girls, drink ourselves stupid. That's the norm. Or it was back then. We never stopped to question why it should be the norm and not the exception.

By then Mom and Dad weren't keeping very strict tabs on me. When I had turned eighteen, my curfew had been extended to midnight. But it wasn't really enforced. When Mom asked me where I had been, I would tell her I had been out with friends. And she would say, "Oh, did you have fun dancing?" I would murmur some words just to get past her as quickly as possible. I think she had in mind some sort of gym dance from my high school days. Thankfully, I don't think she's ever been into a place like Sound Garden, and I hope she never will! In any case, I would cut the conversation short and slope off to bed, keen to hide from her the fact that I was inebriated.

All of this you might classify as initiation into a new and exciting world, the kind of thing that, in my head at least, teenagers were "supposed" to do. The heavy drinking didn't really kick in until I was nineteen. And then came the drugs.

That was when my father died.

Promises and Passing

In the winter of 1997, my father was diagnosed with stage-four cancer. They discovered he had a tumor the size of a lemon in his brain. It came on fast, following a seizure that I had witnessed. It was me who called the ambulance.

I had been awakened from sleep one Saturday morning around 10 a.m., admittedly slightly hung over. Dad walked in without knocking. On his face was an urgency I had never seen before. I knew it was serious when he couldn't formulate any words. The seizure had caused the left side of his face to tremble uncontrollably. I stumbled out of bed, panicked, trying to grasp what was happening, trying to help him but not knowing what to do. It was only after a few fruitless minutes that I reached for the phone and called 9-1-1.

Once the medical personnel had performed several tests to find out what was causing the seizure to his face, an MRI revealed the size and location of the tumor. From the get-go, the doctor gave Dad only six months to live. And being the fighter that he was, he did manage to hold on several months longer than that. Even so, in a life of hard knocks, this was the hardest: the one from which he wouldn't be getting back up. As you might anticipate by now, I didn't know how to handle the sudden onrush of my father's illness and the imminence of his death. I simply didn't have the emotional tools to process it.

By autumn the cancer had spread to his spine. He now had to be in a wheelchair since he had lost all movement in his legs. My memory of that whole period is enveloped in a kind of haze of alternating numbness and pain.

There are only three moments that jump out at me. The first was just over a week before he passed.

My sister Mary and Mom had wheeled him into the living room space onto the rug. The rug was green. Mom loved green. I was in my bedroom next to the living room. My brother Manny was in his bedroom downstairs. Mom hollered out for us to join them in the living room. I remember getting up from my bed, walking slowly.

Manny and I arrived at the doorway together. We edged inside one by one, where Mom positioned us in front of this huddled figure placed in the middle of the room.

He was non-responsive, very sad looking, not moving at all. He just looked empty, devoid of all emotion. It seemed that at this point he had already given up all hope of staying longer. The image of him there remains clear as crystal in my mind, an image that lives with me every day. *The fragility of life*, you might caption it.

"You're going to tell your father that you will continue at school, Mike," said Mom, "how you're going to finish it, right? Go ahead now."

By then I had started college, but my attendance rate was already tailing off. I had just started experimenting with the drug ecstasy, probably only a month before he passed. I couldn't find any words.

"Tell him you're gonna keep doing what you gotta do for your future, Mike."

The same was supposed to apply for Manny, but since he was almost through college by then anyway, mostly this whole setup was for me.

Eventually I found the will to mutter, "Sure, Dad. I'm gonna go to school. I'm gonna go to finish college . . ." although at that point I was almost certain there was no way I would keep this mumbled promise.

Straight after me, Manny blurted out, "Yeah, yeah — I'm gonna keep going. I'm gonna finish too, Dad." My brother looked as uncomfortable as I felt.

After that, I don't remember what happened. The green rug, the cream leather couches, the family pictures scattered about the room, the small figure in the chair . . . it all kind of faded to black.

There was that fight-flight-freeze reaction again that had become my learned response. I had frozen. I couldn't speak, couldn't do anything about it, unable to find the words.

A week later, right before Christmas, we were told it was time to say our goodbyes. By then my other sister, Rosa, was home from where she now lived in Pennsylvania. Mom was sure Dad was going to pass any moment now.

My turn came around. I went into his room, which for a while now had been transformed into something you would see in a hospital, with drips and basins and oxygen tubes and so on around the place. I looked at him lying there. I think his eyes were closed. He wasn't moving at all. I didn't know what to say. With a lurch, I forced myself to step up to the edge of the bed. I grabbed his hand. It was as fragile as a little bird, still warm to the touch. In my head I said simply, "I'm sorry. I'm sorry, Dad." But nothing audible passed my lips.

I felt disconnected, as if I were the inert one, as if someone had pulled the plug on me.

I stood there for a minute, maybe two. I remember the thought that came to me: *Life is very precious.* But somehow it also seemed very cruel. For a man like him to work so hard all his life and then one day he gets told he has cancer and he's dead within the year.

It was a hard thing to see.

Sure enough, my father, Victor Hugo Cabezas, passed away two days later. I think in those two days I had a dream, and in it I bawled my eyes out. It was only when I was conscious that I couldn't let it out. I didn't feel anything because I never had a bond with him. There was nowhere for it to go.

The morning he died, Mom woke me gently to say that he had passed. I got up and went to his room. But then I stopped. I couldn't get past the doorway. I had never seen a dead body before. And that was my last memory of him, as I stood by the doorjamb, peering into the room, watching my sister Patty on the bed hugging his body.

That was December 17, 1998.

The Road Splits

Whether because of my father's death or in spite of it, that time marked a point in the road beyond which I would veer away from the grace that God was calling me to more and more. The voice of conscience was already faint to my ears. From here on for a while I ignored it completely. Doing so led me far off track.

It didn't take too long either.

I had taken my first ecstasy pill about a month before my father passed in a shady underground dance club in New York City. But before long it became a regular feature of any Friday or Saturday night. First there was the anticipation, maybe even a little trepidation. Then came the euphoria, the counterfeit sense of freedom and love, at least for a little while, then the soaring high. I felt my horizons expanding and with them the temptations. Not that any of my friends saw anything wrong with hanging out in clubs on a Friday night, getting high, chasing girls. It wasn't exactly a purpose but at least it was something to do. Once we were into it, we never questioned it.

One occasion, however, gave us good cause to do so. At least it certainly should have in my case.

By now I had turned twenty. There was a group of five of us who would get together regularly at Mark's house or

Dom's, drop a pill (or two), and see where the night would lead.

One night we went over to Mark's house out in Lyndhurst, New Jersey. For some reason, this time we decided to drop ecstasy and stay put rather than head out to the club as normal, where we would be surrounded by others doing the same.

You could say that was taking it a step further.

So, we dropped these pills called "UFOs". Supposedly they came through the same dealer we always got them from, although not directly since Mark had gotten them from a friend. That didn't bother us. Whether from stupidity or naivety, we went right ahead and took them anyway.

We were downstairs in Mark's bedroom listening to trance music, which was what we were into at the time and ideal for this type of drug. There was a small living room space that also led outside. We were chatting away, waiting for the pill to kick in. An hour later, three of the guys were saying they weren't feeling anything right then, nor was I. At this point we figured we had been sold some duds.

"Maybe they're just really weak," suggested Freddy. "We should do another."

Again, stupidity or naivety? It's hard to call which was more to blame.

"Maybe we should wait a bit longer. It's only been an hour.

We don't want to overdo it," said Saul.

But Freddy and Dom went ahead anyway. Saul and I looked at each other, unsure. Saul was always the more cautious one. Meanwhile Mark dropped another, too. Saul and I waited a bit longer, and then I caved . . . and shortly after me, Saul.

Within ten minutes I started feeling really dizzy, feeling this pressure growing and growing in my head. It was not as if it were about to explode; rather, it was more like a feeling of swelling and tightness all over my skull. Meanwhile, I started hallucinating, images flooding my mind every time I closed my eyes.

Saul said he was also feeling weird. The two of us went and sat in the car to listen to music, separating ourselves from the other guys. The music and the images started winding around each other in my head. I was seeing myself walking through clubs, watching girls, noticing people looking at me, hearing the music — as if I were actually there.

Pretty soon I was sick of this situation. I wanted it to end. We went back inside to check on the others. Dom said he was feeling weird, but nothing worse than that. And we ended up sitting on the grass out front waiting for all this to go away.

But it *didn't* go away. It got worse and worse. By now it was two or three in the morning. Saul had to go to work at 7 a.m. I had to be at my brother-in-law's store, where I was working, at 9 a.m. We talked about driving home to try getting some sleep, but neither of us felt we were safe to drive. Instead, we just had to stay put and try letting it pass.

But then from about two o'clock to around five o'clock, we started vomiting, and after that dry-heaving — over and over until I was beyond empty and spewing up flecks of blood.

"Woah, Mikey — you're in a bad way!" said Mark, stating the obvious. "You should probably think about going to the hospital."

"No way! They can't find out I've been doing this stuff." My body now flooded with fear and shame alongside everything else it was trying to deal with. This was about a year after my father had passed. The last thing I needed my family to know, Mom especially, was that I had started taking drugs.

The sun started coming up. We were still out in the grass. No one was tired, of course — that's the whole point. I was still dry heaving up a weird pinkish froth from the pit of my stomach, still seeing crazy visions in my head. I started praying, *God, help me. God, help me,* in my head. *I don't want to do this anymore.*

I was reaching out to him. I knew I was undeserving, but that hardly mattered to me. I was desperate. I needed help (this was one of many prayers of desperation that were to follow).

By 6:30 a.m. Saul felt steady enough to head off to work. He went straight there without any sleep at all. But I still wasn't ready to drive. Around 8 a.m. I got into the car. I was feeling better only since the last half hour. I could at least see now. There were other Sunday morning drivers about. Very cautiously I drove back home to the town where we were now living, a place called Cedar Grove, around twenty minutes away.

I got home. Mom was up. "Where have you been, Mike?"

"Just over at a friend's," I said, ducking through the kitchen as fast as I could before she could see the true state of me. I jumped into the shower, half my mind thanking God that I seemed to be coming out of my "bad trip," half debating whether I should phone my brother-in-law to call in sick or make up some excuse for missing work.

In the end, I did go into the store, looking pretty chewed up, especially on zero sleep. Somehow, I got through my seven-hour shift — don't ask me how — then made it back home and into my bed, where I passed out for about fourteen hours straight.

There's the glamor of taking drugs for you, right there.

It was only God's mercy that stopped it from being a whole lot worse. A lot of kids my age and older have not been so blessed.

Shadows

Of course, for days afterward I told my friends I would never do it again. But then there I was, a mere two weeks later, back at Mark's house with everyone else, dropping pills again. So much for learning my lesson.

This lifestyle went on until around the age of twenty-one, at which point heavy drinking started overtaking the drugs. We would go out to clubs and do shot after shot. You might call it binge drinking. But really, that level of consumption became our new normal.

There was no question that we knew how stupid what we were doing really was. We knew we shouldn't be doing it. But we were like a band of thieves; so long as we all kept doing it together, no one was going to blow the whistle on the game. I guess we weren't so different from a lot of young men and women in that culture at that time.

I would like to believe things are different now, somehow better. I suspect they're not.

So, what did I get out of doing drugs?

One part of it — though not all — was a sort of counterfeit love I would feel when I was on it. There's euphoria during the high, but there's also a feeling of overwhelming love for everyone around you. And you feel as if they love you, too. Of course, it only lasts as long as the chemicals are affecting your brain. It's a delusion, a lie. But for a guy with an unusual deficit of love, a desperate need to feel loved . . . well, maybe that's why I kept going back to it again and again.

But you can't batter the serotonin-producing parts of your brain without some push-back. After all, what goes up must come down, right? And it's probably no surprise to you that before too long the crash came and I entered a long period of depression.

In fact, right from the start the come downs seemed to hit me harder than they did my other friends. I was particularly sensitive to the downswings in mood, which only drives one to repeat the cycle, of course. The deeper you plunge downward, the higher you need to pick yourself up the next time.

I became an obsessive sleeper — a sure sign of depression if you know what you're looking for, but Mom did not, bless her. It wasn't her fault. She had enough going on, trying to cope with the loss of her husband. So, for a while my symptoms went unnoticed. The only medication for my problems came in the form of the weekend highs I administered to myself. It was a period of loneliness and emptiness for sure — even while among my friends we would have told ourselves we were having the time of our lives.

There was a sense of things spiraling out of control.

Sex hadn't yet become part of the problem. That would come later, although around this time I did lose my virginity in an incident so devoid of romance or real pleasure that I'm loath to even relate it to you. Suffice it to say, that seal was broken too. And I was as naive and unguided in the realm of romantic or sexual relationships as I was in every other.

There was a brief flirtation with suicide at this point. At least I entertained suicidal thoughts. Fortunately, recognizing this for what it was — a very bad place at which to have arrived — I was able to reach out to my mother and tell her I wasn't doing so well. Mom, the angel that she is, spoke to a psychologist on my behalf, who prescribed me some antidepressant pills.

Sadly, they didn't help. In fact, they made me feel considerably worse, even a little aggressive, causing me to vent some of the suppressed anger I had built up inside over years of being unable to express my emotions. So, the antidepressants were not a good fit for me (It was only years later that I would discover this drug had a serious side effect that tended to increase the incidence of suicide in its users. Eventually it was pulled from the market).

This seesaw existence — between the artificial highs of partying and drugs and alcohol on one hand and the lows of loneliness and depression and anger on the other — couldn't go on forever. After two or three years, I became increasingly withdrawn, pulling back from the socializing and partying of the period immediately following my father's death. I reverted into my teenage bubble of staying home and playing video games. Sometimes I would play for eight or nine hours straight in a day.

Probably that would have gone on for a long time were it not for an unlikely lifeline that dragged me back toward some semblance of purpose for my life:

Krauszer's Food Store & Deli.

A Lifeline

All through this time I had been attending Essex County Community College, where I had been enrolled first in a liberal arts program before later switching to business management. I wasn't exactly the model student. As my personal problems had gotten worse, so had my attendance record until I dropped from full-time to part-time study.

Meanwhile I was working for my brother-in-law Darryl, who owned Krauszer's Food Store & Deli on Franklin Street in Belleville. Darryl was married to my eldest sister, Patty. He's eighteen years older than me, so while he didn't exactly represent a father figure to me — nor did he ever try to be — he *was* a sympathetic adult willing to speak into my life. He had given me the job of helping at the store, but he also now gave me a real incentive.

He told me that if I worked hard and proved that I really wanted it, he would give me the opportunity of buying into the store business. His motto was *Work hard; play hard,* which sounded good to me, although I don't suppose either of us asked himself to what end, any more than most do who live by those words. Still, I will always remain grateful to Darryl for the opportunity — because I can see now how much having this goal helped me out of a real swamp of inertia. It gave me something to focus my attention on, something substantial. Something real.

That's not to say that this was necessarily the right choice for me at the time. But it was a way out, an escape from that other life. It was this semblance of responsibility that enabled me to climb out of my depression. From the age of twenty-one through twenty-three, I worked mostly full time in Krauszer's. As it happens, I did finish college; I did keep my promise to my dying father (but that would come later) — which *is* important to me. By then, however, academics had settled for a distant second place to the "real-world" opportunity I was already working toward.

By the time my twenty-fourth birthday came around, in April 2004, I had saved enough money to add to what I had borrowed from Mom and to buy into Darryl's business. I was to have a 33.3-percent share. We signed the contract in July 2004.

I was officially now a businessman. I had a proper income. I had prospects and a future. I could hold up my head as a person of substance.

And I was about to fall in love for the first time in my life. Perhaps now, at last, things would be different.

CHAPTER FOUR

Counterfeit Gods

If we look to some created thing to give us the meaning, hope, and happiness that only God himself can give, it will eventually fail to deliver and will break our hearts. - Tim Keller

Her name was Gabriella.

I met her in a friend's bar in the Ironbound district of Newark. Back then this was predominantly the Portuguese, Brazilian, and Spanish part of the city. It had a certain flavor, if you can call it that. If anything, it's become more Brazilian now.

It was a small place, a corner bar. I can't remember how we were introduced — whether we just got to talking or someone else was there. I discovered she was half French, half Portuguese, which even now seems impossibly exotic for a place like that. My world was rocked; she was stunningly beautiful. Of course, I asked her if I could see her again. She gave me the address of the place she was working: a big new club that had just opened in the Ironbound called the XL Lounge, where it turned out she was a VIP service bottle girl. She was there to add a touch of glamor to the place. And *glamor* was the right word in its archaic sense: instantly, she had cast a spell over me. I was enthralled.

The following week I went over there with a couple of friends. She was working and showed us to a table. There was some flirting, some kidding around, and when she came back with our drinks, I asked her out on a date — the first time I had ever done anything like that, let alone in front of my friends.

I remember Depeche Mode playing in the background, her peering at me with a surprised look on her face, as if she were blown away that I would just flat-out ask her. But believe me,

she wasn't nearly as surprised as I was. This was the first time I had really wanted something so badly, had still felt somewhat intimidated, but instead of shrinking away, I had stepped up to the plate, sipped down the rest of my drink, some liquid courage coursing through my veins. I was bold. And it paid off.

In my head I was looking at the girl of my dreams and she had just said yes. I couldn't believe my luck.

She gave me her number and told me to call her to set up a date. After that, I hung out for a little longer in the club drinking with my friends. And I remember that feeling on the way home that night, basking in the "glory" of knowing that for the first time in my life I had shown I was a real man. I had swallowed my fear, gone ahead and shot for the moon, and succeeded. She was dazzling. And she had said yes. It felt like my first real taste of manhood.

That was how it started. And it didn't take long for me to fall head-over-heels in love with this woman.

Pretty soon it was all about the nightlife, all about the glamor, and it was as if she, Gabriella, was the embodiment of it all. I had decent money in my pocket. I had this gorgeous woman on my arm. Those shabby days of popping pills were behind me. Now it was all expensive liquor, sharp clothes, a nice watch, a fancy car (a seventy-grand Lexus, no less.)

Hey, I was finally moving up in the world! That's what I told myself. And that was how the world started to treat me. It fed my confidence. That old itch of needing attention was being scratched good and hard, and it felt great. I'll not deny it.

Of course, the confidence that all this gave me was just as counterfeit as the fake euphoria of taking ecstasy. But it was going to take me a long time to realize that.

Beauty

Beautiful as she was, Gabriella had a cocaine habit even before I met her. But I could hardly point the finger. Much of my inflated confidence was fueled by alcohol. It was the culture I was moving in, but also the crutch that held me up.

Yes, alcohol was my crutch.

But love was my counterfeit god. Love was going to save me. Love was worth every sacrifice. Love was the higher power to whom I was willing to give my soul. And Gabriella was the altar on which I would lay it all down.

As one famous rock band once sang, "All you need is love."

Turns out they were wrong.

I found out about Gabriella's cocaine habit late one night while she was working at the club. It was after hours, around 3 a.m. I turned up to see her in the bar. As I ordered a drink, I asked the bartender where she was.

"She's out back doing a couple lines with the others." She said it casually but then must have seen the shocked expression on my face. This was another level of worldliness, if you like, for me. I didn't know anyone for whom that was so normal. But it turned out everyone in the place was doing it. This was a Thursday night. I felt at once impossibly naive, like a deer in headlights, and yet it was obvious I was supposed to take it in stride, to "be cool" about it. In truth, I felt vulnerable, being exposed to this next revelation of the world's fallenness. Sure, I had taken drugs myself, so you might think, *Why the surprise?* But I guess it was seeing the normalization of it that troubled me. From then on, I realized that every time we were out and Gabriella went to the bathroom, she was often doing a line. My reaction to this was that I suddenly saw myself as her knight in shining armor. I wanted to save her.

But she wasn't really buying it. She tried cutting back, even giving it up. But not that hard.

Meanwhile, a clear state of codependence was developing between us without either of us realizing it. At the time I certainly didn't see it that way. To me, Gabriella was this sophisticated woman of the world who was expanding my horizons as much as she was bolstering my image to that world. We went to places I never would have dreamed of going around New York City and New Jersey. That's why I was so in love with her, I told myself. She was breaking down the walls of my limited little world, showing me what was possible. The coke was simply a part of this new landscape of sophistication, even though I didn't like it.

Now that I think of it, with her beside me I tended to drink less than I otherwise would. Who needs the false confidence that five or six cocktails can give you when you already have the most beautiful woman in the room on your arm?

As for the sex, she was as sophisticated in the bedroom as she was everywhere else. Being far more experienced than me in that area, she led me on a journey of discovery, introducing me to experiences and feelings that I had hardly dreamed were possible (after all, up to this point everything I knew in the realm of sex had come straight out of a porn magazine). It was intoxicating. *She* was intoxicating. And I started telling myself, *this is who I am, too. This is the real me emerging like a butterfly from its cocoon.*

I had no clue, no sense at the time, that very slowly, very subtly I would soon lose my true self in her completely. I didn't notice that I was only adapting myself to whatever she was doing or whatever she wanted me to be. It never went the other way. I was imitating her lifestyle, her interests, her way of being in the world.

As the old patriarchs so often warned, worship an idol for long enough and you end up becoming that idol.

What was the idol exactly? You could call it beauty, or you could call it love — a sort of abstract notion, a goal to pursue. Gabriella became the embodiment of those things, even while Gabriella the actual person faded into the background. But you can't worship that which is not truly worthy. It was not because Gabriella wasn't a perfectly decent woman but rather because there is only one who is worthy, and that is God, Himself. Worship anything less than our creator and it will first disappoint you and finally break you.

Sounds a little dramatic?

I can assure you that we're all doing it, all the time. As the British writer G. K. Chesterton wrote, "When we cease to worship God, we don't worship nothing. We worship anything."

And if we run too far with that worship, we are in danger of losing our very selves. So, while I felt that I was "discovering" my true self as our relationship unfolded, the very opposite was true. I was constructing a counterfeit self in the image of the woman I worshiped. I was moving away from the truth, not toward it.

False image. False self.

None of this was Gabriella's fault, of course. It was merely my response to her.

She had immigrated to the United States and come to live in Newark around ten years before. Her father was French, and her mother was Portuguese. She had learned English fluently while living in America. She had a natural class about her, being well-mannered and proper. She still presented herself much more like a European than an American, certainly not one from Newark. At the same time, there was something a little mysterious about her (perhaps there always is the first time you really fall in love).

Right from the start it was very romantic between us. Flowers, classy restaurants, picnics, little gifts, and love notes. I was all in for that. I had to up my game. But upping my game meant really playing at being someone I was not. Then again, being yourself isn't easy either if you have no solid idea of who that person is.

Maybe that was the difference between us. Her personality felt as if it were already strongly formed and defined. Mine was still very malleable. Even that may be an illusion. More likely, she was just as lost as the rest of us.

The truth is that our relationship didn't last that long, only six months. But that was long enough to lose my soul and break my heart when the end came. The irony is that I couldn't deal with the fact that she was a heavy cocaine user. And even though I tried to lead her away from it, it was only getting worse. I suggested getting help through church — believe it or not, I still went from time to time — and then through a psychologist. But all this was far more about me not liking her doing it than her embarrassing herself or suffering any serious medical condition and wanting to quit. The incentive to stop was mine, not hers. And sure enough, she became more secretive about using it, becoming harder to track down. Trust between us dissolved. These days you might call it "ghosting" or "gaslighting" as she would not respond to calls and texts for two days, sometimes three. And then out of the blue she would suddenly reply as if nothing had changed. It would mess with my head and my heart.

She was pulling away, and the more she did so the more I allowed myself to be sucked right in after her — until eventually even I reached my limit. The writing was on the wall. I had to cut her off.

I spent the next two and a half weeks sobbing into my pillow, discovering for the first time what so many do: that love hurts — probably more than it needed to, and certainly more than I ever expected.

The idol was broken. And I lay in pieces right beside it.

Sex

Afterwards came the next pivot, away from drugs and drink for a while and toward people, or more specifically, toward women and sex. I was no longer looking for "love" if all that love could give me was a broken heart. But the thrill of sex, of the endless availability of beautiful women out there in the glittering city — that was now where I sought my fulfilment.

But it was not just fulfilment but affirmation again, the same bottomless pit that I had tried to fill with singing and fooling around in class and baseball all those years before — the same thirst that could not be slaked. But, boy, did I try!

If a woman was willing to choose me, even if it was only for a night, I would take it. Contradiction was at the heart of it all. On the one hand I continued holding on to this perfect image in my head of meeting the right girl, settling down, living happily ever after. And on the other hand, I would spend my nights on the hunt for women looking to party, no strings attached.

I was twenty-six. The first of my friends were already starting to find partners for life. I didn't want to get left behind. So, after a period of raw promiscuity, I did start dating women a little more seriously. And if they didn't have an explicit drug problem, I could tolerate quite a lot, all kinds of behavior, some of which you might call abusive. But I had watched Mom take a lot from my father over the years. I must have figured, *that's what you have to do in a relationship to make things work — stick at it through thick and thin.* But really it meant jettisoning my self-respect — at least at times. I was the accommodating one. I was the one bending over backwards. I was the one twisting myself way out of shape to fit who they were.

Most of these I would call "mini relationships": two, three, or maybe even four month affairs that all trailed away into nothing after a time. They started feeling meaningless. And so, my attention started falling back on myself. What was I going to do? How was I going to make my mark in this world?

Turned out a pretty big change was coming.

Money

Maybe money could do what love and sex could not. Maybe money could be my purpose, my guide, my savior. Maybe, to steal Brando's line, I could be a contender.

I was already proud of myself that at twenty-four I had become a business owner — and not just any business but one that actually made good money, money that could change my lifestyle for the better. There was a little bit of the American dream creeping in there.

Up to this point, the first few years of my twenties, I hadn't been that close to my brother, Manny. We hadn't fallen out or anything, but he had been going through his own stuff, facing his own challenges, which although regrettable were unsurprising given our family history. He is almost four years older than me, but I never felt that he was someone to turn to as I tried unsuccessfully to navigate romantic relationships. I'm not saying he didn't try. But remember, I was trying to be someone I wasn't, my own little god, you could say.

Even if the desire had been there to love someone well and in a lasting way, I had no idea of how to do that. The best I had to guide me were glossy lifestyle mags like *Men's Health* and *GQ*, these aspirational image factories that really were completely unrealistic and unhelpful. Yet somehow, they would convince you that if you buy their magazines and follow their advice, you could be a sex god in the bedroom, a rock star on the clubbing scene, and a hotshot tycoon in the boardroom, the trading floor, or wherever. It was mostly nonsense, but if you paid the subscription, they were ready to keep the dream alive.

We would stock these kinds of magazines in the store, and while it's a bit depressing to admit it, they became my go-to reference library for living. There was a new explosion of promiscuity at that time, the late nineties and early "naughties." It was nothing in the dating scene across New Jersey and New York to be seeing two, three, four girls at a time, even more, probably sleeping with all of them if you could get away with it.

Friends was the popular TV show at the time, together with the spicier *Sex and the City*. That was how it was done: casual dating, casual sex, looking for "hookups" only. After all, you didn't want to be tied down to one option when a better one might walk around the corner any moment. Commitment somehow became unfashionable, and the fact that people's feelings got trampled on in the process wasn't your problem. "I never created any expectations" — that was always the justification. "I always said it was casual."

Looking back, I find it amazing that anyone found lasting love in all that mess.

So, what was a *real* man supposed to look like?

Men's Health would tell you. *FHM* and *Esquire,* too. Maybe this was what was feeding into the next phase of my life. I was driving a Lexus convertible, I was dating Brazilian "models" who were wildcats in bed, I was splashing cash in the best clubs around town. The editors of *GQ* would've been proud. If they presented me with a box to tick, I was right there, pen in hand.

It's a big world out there, I remember thinking, *and I'm going to make the most of it.* I was going to drink from every cup. And though I couldn't have known it at the time, this was *the world* pulling me closer.

Most have heard of the Trinity — Father, Son, and Holy Spirit. But there is such a thing as the *un*holy trinity too: the flesh, the devil, and the world. This was the last of those, slipping its coils around me, seeping its poison into my blood very seductive, very hard to resist, especially when you have money to burn and no compelling reason to steer clear.

And at the time I had made that link in my head: if I can make more money, I can have more of this stuff — faster cars, flashier apartments, sexier girls, shinier toys.

Money, I need more money.

As it happens, that was the path about to open to me.

I had no inkling that this was going to lead me even farther away from God. Even if I had, I don't think it would have stopped me.

Everything was too easy. Life wasn't meant to be like this. You weren't supposed to be able to log online to some random website, represent yourself as "looking for a serious relationship" (which, to be honest, all parties knew was crazy), turn up at a stranger's apartment, drink a cup of the devil's cocktail, and then have sex. The low bar to self-gratification was of no help to young men whatsoever (nor to young women, I imagine. But that's for someone else to speak to, not me).

How much better to know you win the girl and the goodies only once you've proven yourself worthy of them — when you've worked hard and demonstrated yourself to be a man of your word, a man of integrity, a man of good conscience, a man who's gonna stick. Then, if you were lucky, someone might marry you. *Then* you get the goodies.

We had it all backwards then. I think we still do.

What we lost was purpose, identity, fulfilment, all while we told ourselves we had it all. The sexual revolution of the sixties and seventies was supposed to empower women and liberate men. All it did was create more division, more confusion, and it created a new generation of sex addicts, lesser versions of what we could be.

It was another lie we all swallowed.

Professionally I was managing partner of Krauzser's store, in business with my brother-in-law. That was going well most of the time. I looked up to Darryl, at least from a business point of view. He was a great negotiator. I learned a lot from him. But I never went to him for any advice outside of business, nothing personal. He saw the way I was partying hard. I guess the most he ever said was "If you're going to play hard, you've got to work hard too." I will never forget that. But as a philosophy, it can't take you very far, even though there is merit in the idea that working hard at whatever you do is always non-negotiable.

I still had my buddy, Saul. He was a great listener, but he was never one for coming up with strong advice. Besides, we were the same age, trying to figure out life together. He wasn't in such a different position as me.

Apart from that, I had zero people to confide in, no source of wisdom to steer me through the next stretch of the road, barely any source of experience either. Mom was there in support. But even she had a limited perspective. What did she know about advising a young man with his pockets full of money as to how to make his way in twenty-first-century America?

And God . . . I guess He was still there, allowing me to go and play in the street, so to speak. And that's exactly what I was doing. Little did I know I was about to get hit by a car.

Several cars, in fact.

As far as I was concerned, I was living the life of a successful man. So, when the opportunity came along, it felt like a natural progression for "that guy."

I jumped on it with both hands.

It came about because Saul's father owned a liquor license that he wanted to sell. He also had a space in the Ironbound district that up till that point he had set up as a bar. I still remember the day Saul walked into the store with his, attractive Brazilian girlfriend on his arm — that should have been a red flag right there since he was hugely under her influence. He told me he had a business opportunity for me.

His plan was to open a restaurant. My first reaction was to say no. I had my hands full with the store. Instead, I suggested that he ask my brother, Manny, since he had just graduated from a French culinary institute and was working a tough gig as a sous-chef in New York City. This was a golden opportunity for Manny, carte blanche, as it were, to run his own kitchen nearly straight out of chef school.

Saul and Manny talked. We all talked some more. And eventually I found myself drawn into the plan with the two of them. So that became the dynamic and we started plotting how we were going to do this. The top line was this: it was going to take a whole lot of money. Our initial estimate of how much we would need was something between $350,000 to $450,000.

This was the first question, then. How could we raise the money to buy in?

Of course, the unspoken driver for all this was the same one that had been there in my classroom, in the sanctuary at church: I was going to *be somebody*. The glamor of a fresh, cool new restaurant in an up-and-coming part of town, and it was going to be "our joint." That felt pretty good, I'm not gonna lie.

We had big plans. We thought we were going to be millionaires within five years. Hey, at least you couldn't fault our optimism. But as I look back, it's too easy to see that we were going into it for the wrong reasons. We were going to make a name for ourselves. We were going to be people whom folks wanted to know. But that was the problem. We were too focused on the cherry on top when we didn't yet have much of a clue about how to bake the cake. But that was the world we were swimming in: it was all about the show. The bling. The two-thousand-dollar suits from Brooks Brothers. Why not? I had to look the part, right? After all, I was going to be the face of the restaurant. Manny was going to be head chef, of course. And Saul would be the bar manager. We all had titles. But as you'll see, what good are titles if you can't follow through on them?

Most of the money, from Manny and my side at least, came from Mom. She put her house on a home equity loan to lend us what we needed. It was so incredibly generous of her. She deserves more than an honorary mention here. She went beyond the extra mile for her boys, raising $300,000 for us.

I wish I could say we honored her trust, that we were worthy of her sacrifice. But the truth is that having that money enabled us to make more stupid mistakes, to do more of the craziness we were already into, than allowing us the opportunity of our dreams.

We launched in the early fall of 2008. I was twenty-nine years old. Manny was thirty-two. Saul was the same age as me. We had invited the city mayor to come for the grand opening and had photographs taken of us shaking his hand for the local newspaper. It was a big deal. There were council members and other local politicians drinking cocktails at the opening party. This was how it was supposed to be. So we figured.

Our architect was well connected. His architectural firm was in the heart of downtown Newark, New Jersey, so his contacts helped us off to a strong start. We called the place Misavi — *MI-SA-VI* being the first two letters of each of our names (recall that Manny's first name was Victor).

And so . . . we got to work.

It was soon obvious that two-thousand-dollar suit or not, overseeing the floor of a restaurant was going to be incredibly demanding. I immediately found myself running this way and that, obliging the patrons, liaising between the kitchen and front of house, checking the bar, having small talk with the patrons again, lending a hand serving dishes. It was nothing less than an intense wake-up call. If I'm honest, I must admit that I had had no idea what it would entail, no forewarning of how exhausting, how stressful it would all be.

It didn't take long before I had ditched the suit, opting instead for simple black pants and a button-up shirt, realizing that I was going to have to get my hands dirty.

The place itself was newly renovated. We had done it up in red and white in a contemporary style: white walls, red glass panels around the counters, white tables and chairs, white leather lounge sofas, glass tiles on the bar. It seated about sixty people with standing room for another two hundred — so not huge — divided between an eating area and a bar area. The name "Misavi" appeared in a logo on the floor, frosted into the glass entrance. It looked cool, actually.

The cuisine was all down to my brother. He came up with the idea that it should be "New American fusion." That was a brand-new concept back then, bringing together American and Spanish cuisines. I remember he wanted to make it into a kind of tapas place, but in the end, we opted for full-blown entrées. At least that was the direction we took, thinking we could make more money that way.

Word started getting out. People started coming. The old itch was getting scratched. I felt like somebody people wanted to pay attention to, wanted to know — the women especially, if I'm honest.

We had designed a beautiful place, and now it was full of beautiful people. It was exciting. It was classy. Everyone said so.

We had arrived at last.

The counterfeit gods were smiling down on us. And like grinning fools, we smiled right back.

CHAPTER FIVE

An Idol Falls

The desire for fame tempts even noble minds.
- Saint Augustine

The rudest awakening to us was how exhausting it was to service a place like Misavi, how much energy it took out of us just to make it all run smoothly. We were open seven days a week — sixteen-solid-hour days. But at least in late 2008 the prices we could charge were still high. We were making money, at least for a short time.

Then the first wave of the financial crash rolled through. Bear Stearns had already failed in March of that year. Lehman Bros failed around the time we launched. The downswing wasn't long in coming after that. It suddenly became clear that we had bought into the hospitality business at the top of the market and that the only way from there was down — barring a miracle.

People lost their 401(k)s and consequently stopped going out as much. And even when they were out, they wouldn't spend as much. They simply didn't have the cash.

In response, we revamped the menu so that it did come to look more like a tapas place. But even that wasn't enough. Once the recession was in full swing, we had to pivot again into something that was more like a straight-up bar and lounge club.

The stress of adapting to the increasingly hostile winds of the market took its toll on Manny, especially because he was responsible for the menu, and in every way, he was more experienced than all of us. Under that kind of pressure, the easiest thing to do is self-medicate. Alcohol was our medicine of choice to combat the stress.

Looking back, I should have noticed. I should have had his back. I don't know why I couldn't. Was the situation looming like that bully from the sidewalk? *You are a worthless person. What are you gonna do about it?* Or was it the serpent's deceitful illusion? *You, too, can be like gods . . .*

Sooner or later, we had to face the stark reality that we weren't making money anymore.

For me, the financial stress of that wasn't as impactful because I was still getting income from my holding in Krauzser's. But working two jobs was physically shattering. Darryl had given me six months to focus on Misavi, during which I took a cut in profits, but as that period drew to an end, he expected me to pick up the reins again. I found I was working seventy, eighty, even ninety hour weeks — locking up Misavi at 3 a.m., snatching an hour or so of rest before being up to open the store at 5 a.m.

It was no way to live.

Saul and Manny were working hours nearly as long and for far less money too, since the idea was that we would continue reinvesting back into the business the money we made. Essentially, we were all in the same boat. Relations between us all began to get fractious, especially between those two. Manny was responsible for the kitchen and food. Saul was supposed to be managing the bar and alcohol. The financial noose was tightening on all of us. But Saul, bless him . . . try as he might, he was able to give only to the limit of his capacity. All of us were stretched, but we were having to deal with the ugly truth that this venture was way beyond our pay grade. Put simply, we had gotten into the business for the wrong reasons.

Despite our collective burden, the overall financial health of the company was my responsibility. And to be honest, I too, was already way outside my experience and comfort zone. These were uncharted waters to me and far harder to navigate than I had anticipated.

The pressure built and built for all of us, and we all reacted differently, none of us well. The whole culture of the place did us no favors. Misavi had evolved, out of necessity, from a smart contemporary American fusion restaurant into essentially a lounge club in a few short months. There was a DJ in the larger space in the corner of the restaurant. The liquor license ran to 3 a.m., which at least meant we could make more money. But it changed the vibe of the place. People were drinking a lot more. The three of us were drinking a lot too, with access to as much free booze as we wanted. The club vibe was attracting a different kind of clientele. It was less about the food now and more about the bar takings.

And now people were bringing in drugs too.

With less emphasis on the food and with my having to spend more time in the store, Manny shifted from working in the kitchen to the bar. That was a big change, and not for the better, certainly not for him. I should have voiced my concerns to him. I should have been a better brother to him, just as I should have been a better friend to Saul. My failure on both fronts has haunted me for years. But I was struggling myself — reticent, pivoting inward. So, I just ignored their problems, not knowing how to deal with them or help them through it all.

Again, that lack of confrontation reared its head. I didn't speak up when I should have. I didn't know how.

Drowning

Meanwhile, I had gotten into another relationship — the next one that really meant anything — with a woman named Lydia. We had met when I was out scouting for service and bartending talent in a club called the Vivo Lounge. Like Gabriella before her, Lydia was working as a bottle girl there in the VIP section. I approached her and told her that we were opening a bar in the Ironbound district and asked if she were interested in getting a little extra part-time work. We exchanged Facebook details and soon were connected. That was the beginning. And the relationship soon became more than merely professional.

Lydia was as smart as she was bubbly and beautiful. She didn't come over to us at once. She was too canny for that. But once she had decided the place had something to it, she came to work for us (I think liking me had something to do with it as well).

Pretty quickly she came to occupy an important role in the business besides her being my girlfriend. She had ideas and vision, especially when it came to upselling around the bar. She proved a huge asset to us. She knew how to make money out of customers based on her years of experience doing just that at the Vivo Lounge. It's fair to say that the business endured a lot longer because of her.

Everything about her seemed like a good fit to me. She was attractive, intelligent, and business savvy. It wasn't long before I asked her to move in with me. As with Gabriella, I was idealizing the relationship, playing it forward in my head to the happy ending as I was in some romantic movie. I leaned far too heavily on it too soon, diving into a level of codependence almost immediately, long before the relationship had proved strong and steady.

We were together for two years. But it started getting toxic long before that. Again, it was because I didn't have the backbone to say what needed to be said. I would just let things go. And by letting things slide, I became complicit in their downfall.

The bar business continued dwindling with grim inevitability. We were sinking fast. I couldn't help feeling as though I had taken charge of a ship that had leaks right from the get-go. As they say, hindsight is 20/20. Ultimately, I said nothing to Saul, nothing to Manny, which is not to say that it didn't bother me. It did. Everything did. I was filling up with resentment and frustration at how everything was unravelling. And yet I just let it all pass almost without comment.

To quell the powerful emotions inside, I turned to the bottle more and more. The fact is that all of us were drowning in more ways than one.

The background pressure that was always there was, of course, all the money we had poured into the business. I was making the payments on our loan every month both for Manny and for me. I had taken on the responsibility for paying the minimum due. After all, I had the store income. It was still unbelievably stressful. $225,000 each, as the initial investment. That's a heck of a lot of money when you can't see any way of making it back.

The breaking point had to come soon. Between us. Within us.

Already I knew this idol was broken and fast becoming unsalvageable. But the question was: How long could we hang on before it broke us too?

The image I had created for myself was melting right before my eyes.

Reality was revealing itself to me, even though I wasn't aware of it at the time—the emptiness of living apart from God, the futility of the goals that we build up for ourselves to pursue, thinking they are going to lead to fulfilment and meaning and satisfaction, how ultimately, they betray us and God's good plan for us. Meanwhile God in His grace lets us break ourselves against these false idols. And then He says, *Well, are you ready now?* wasn't. Not yet.

When Idols Break

In the latter half of 2009 we were getting more and more party people in Misavi. That meant folks into heavier drinking and harder drugs. Meanwhile, Manny and I swapped so that I spent more time at the back of the house now and he was running the bar area out front. He did this to relieve his younger brother of a burden I was increasingly unable to handle — not to mention to save me from certain burnout. I guess that's what brothers are supposed to do for each other, lay down their own lives for each other.

We had switched because my hours at the store would no longer allow me to work late nights. I just couldn't sustain shutting down the club last thing at night (which was technically early morning) and then getting into the store to open up at the crack of dawn. As it was, I was irritable and edgy all the time for lack of sleep. Besides drinking more, I started gravitating more towards "uppers" like amphetamine salts just to keep me functional. That would at least keep me awake when I needed to be. And somehow, I managed to convince myself that I would be able to handle it all: the pressure of "running" two businesses, a codependent girlfriend, my brother and best friend coming to their wits end. Of course, I was massively deluding myself. I told myself this was what it took to run a lounge bar and club. I didn't want to admit to myself what is obvious to me now: that the business was failing.

Meanwhile, I was trying to keep Lydia happy, telling her I was all in, that we were heading for marriage. But that was a promise I knew I couldn't keep. I told her I would get out of the business to spend more time with her — another empty promise.

As for Misavi, I convinced the others that if we put more money into it, we could save it. I must have been wound tight. On one DJ opening night we were short-staffed, and I was bartending. There was a guy who had had too much to drink who slammed down his drink on the bar and smashed the glass. In the blink of an eye, I was over the bar and had this guy in a chokehold. The bouncer had to pull me off him. It was a total overreaction but symptomatic of what I was feeling inside — this tightly wound coil of rage and frustration and worry.

On that occasion the police were called. The cops who showed up were friends of mine, and we were outside by then. My cop friends tried to keep me away from the other guy. He was denying everything, saying it was all my fault, an unprovoked attack. Somehow for a few moments my friends' attention was directed elsewhere, and I squared up to the guy and confronted him. He was still denying he had done anything wrong, and so without any warning I clocked him. He went down heavy.

It was not good. I wasn't even drunk. I was angry, stressed, worn so incredibly thin. The cops had to pull me out of the situation a second time.

I was lucky the guy didn't press charges. He was very, very drunk, so who knows how much he remembered? It turned out he had been drinking all night with his friends before he even got to our place.

Another situation proved to be the icing on the cake. One night my good friend got mixed up in a brawl outside the bar. Of course, everyone that night had had too much to drink. I was closing the registers inside. My friends had mostly left by then, except for a few. One guy in particular, Ryan, had gotten into an altercation with a girl outside and she had slapped him. I don't know the particulars of what was said or why, only that Ryan had slapped her back. Little did he know or maybe he did and just didn't care — that she was with her boyfriend and two other guys. See, Ryan is a former Iraqi war veteran and tough as they come. He and I had been close for a couple years at that point.

Saul told me Ryan was getting in a fight outside. Immediately I stopped what I was doing and ran out to find him, still in my fancy suit. I saw him being kicked and punched on the ground. I charged over. But then somehow, I hesitated, hovering over him in a feeble attempt to break up their attack. They were raging, though, and kept on. Once again I froze with the cold realization that even in this extreme situation, I couldn't rouse myself to protect my friend.

I think I reasoned that if I weighed in, the business (and my partners) would be adversely affected by my involvement. When his attackers were sated and it was all over, it was someone else who picked Ryan off the floor and took him away. The cops had been called so most others were leaving too. All in all, it was a grubby little event making life harder with our neighbors, bringing unwanted attention from the city of Newark authorities, and even resulting in a brick through our window the following night. Of course, my friendship with Ryan would never be the same. He knew I had failed him. Another casualty of the chaos I had created for myself.

Was this God's plan for my life? I knew it couldn't be. It felt as though I had gone far off the rails and bowed down to that snake in the garden. Now I was spitting out the seeds from all that forbidden fruit — no longer sweet but bitter as poison. Much like my life had come to feel that way.

Eventually I took a few days off to go visit Montreal. I told Manny and Saul that if I didn't, I was going to end up in a mental institution or something. That's how bad it was.

That was only midway through 2009. On those few days I was already thinking that we had to sell the place. In fact, we kept going well into 2011. I had thought maybe we could save it when my brother-in-law Darryl considered buying Saul's share for a hundred thousand if memory serves right. He had grand designs on how he could restructure and save the place. But he and Manny couldn't find their way to an agreement and eventually Darryl pulled away.

We were truly in fight-flight-or-freeze mode as the thing started imploding.

In 2010 I told the others that I was going to put Misavi up for sale and see what happened. While this went ahead, my relationship with Lydia was in freefall. We were arguing all the time, and it just didn't seem possible to separate the downfall of the business from the disintegration of my private life, probably because Lydia was working at Misavi as well. So, she could see the chaos and collapse of what was happening there. On the one hand, she needed a partner who was present for her — and at the same time she needed her space from me. She was getting neither. I was just a fractious, angry man who didn't know what to do to save the situation. She started calling me out on legitimate things: too much drinking, not giving her the attention she deserved. There are moments, even now, when I wonder whether things could have worked out with Lydia if I hadn't been in such a state. Then I remember this one scene: we were arguing, and she came at me and pushed me. Then I grabbed her and shoved her back. Her legs caught the couch and she fell back onto it.

It was an ugly moment. Aggressive. Not me, not who I am. And yet it must have frightened her. It certainly scared me. It couldn't go on. None of it.

By late 2010 both Manny and Saul had all but pulled out of the business. They were off looking for other work and Darryl put more pressure on me to give up one thing or the other: Misavi or the store. I even started getting pressure from my family, Mom and my sisters, to put an end to the misery.

So, one day I found a realtor to put up the restaurant for sale. It was clear that most of the money we had invested was going to be lost. We managed to recoup only around a hundred thousand. We had lost over half a million dollars. There was a brief interim period when we tried to recoup some losses by subleasing it to another group. But that also ended in a mess. By then the place itself had become seedy. There were late-night call girls working out of there and a lot of drug dealing happening on and around the property. On one occasion a stabbing almost occurred.

In the end I had to go through the headache of evicting those people who had refused to sign a contract in the first place (never a good sign, but we were on the ropes). When they left, it was a mess.

We finally sold the liquor license and the leasehold in the first months of 2011. By then, Saul and Manny had long jumped ship, saying only that whatever money I could salvage from the situation was good.

Lydia had left me too. To be honest, she had been entirely honorable throughout the whole demise of the business. And there had been a moment during it all when Manny had taken me aside and told me that I should hang on to her, that a woman like her doesn't come along very often. I didn't listen. And so, I lost her too.

It was a lot to deal with. A lot to lose.

I can only thank God that I still had the store, and that Darryl was someone stable on whom I could rely. Without that, I would have been entirely lost.

Perhaps I should have listened to Darryl in the first place. I remember his telling me that 80 percent of restaurant start-ups were destined to fail. That's in the first three years. Of course, aged twenty-nine and feeling invincible, I just figured that others might fail — but not us.

Well, I paid the price for my hubris.

By the time it was all over I was turning thirty-one years old, was single and broke, and looked like a zombie.

Another God Rises

As one idol lay fallen and smashed into a thousand pieces on the ground, another was about to make an unexpected appearance, one I couldn't have foreseen. It was going to have perhaps an even more profound effect on my self-made image.

My health was not good at this time. I had been through the wringer, mentally, emotionally, and with so little sleep and so little care of my body, physically too. But even though I felt like a physical wreck, I was determined that this setback would not finish me. I refused to be taken out. I was still going to make something of myself.

Meanwhile, I had gone to the doctor for a checkup, and when he saw the state I was in, decided he needed to do some blood tests. Sure enough, the blood samples went off and a while later the report came back saying various hormone levels were down. I think it was a deficiency of iron, or something to do with my liver. But the young doctor who was seeing me — he was only a few years older than I was — asked me whether I felt lethargic often. Did I feel weak? How was I sleeping? And so on.

He walked me through the report and then laid down his pen. "Do you want to see whether a testosterone supplement would help you?"

I hesitated. "I don't know. I . . . it doesn't feel like something I should be going on."

"Oh, but it'll give you more energy. You'll feel stronger in your major muscle groups. You'll sleep far better." He laughed. "You'll feel like you're twenty-one again."

I could feel the sell. But I allowed him to push me, just as I always had. "I suppose I could give it a go."

He filled out a prescription. And even as I took it to the pharmacy, I had this little doubt scratching in my head. *Should I be doing this?*

I'll never forget it. Afterwards I went to the doctor again, and he offered to show me how to inject myself in my thigh. I remember him drawing the liquid into the syringe, the little squirt, then calmly pinning me just above my knee. Then he said, "Just like that."

"Right. How often?"

"Once a week . . . for the rest of your life." "What?" I blurted.

"Of course. This is not a short-term thing," he explained. "You do this as long as you need to. Once your body adjusts, these synthetic injections become a substitute for your own natural testosterone production."

I just let him do it. And this was the "gateway drug" to much more serious stuff—anabolic steroids and so on, which as you'll see, were connected to my next attempt to construct an image for myself, the next lie I would set myself to pursue.

It would lead into the world of fitness, modelling, a pageant competition . . . and ultimately to the very door of death.

CHAPTER SIX

Face to Face with the Shadow

Refusing to be average can be a very costly thing.
- M.A.C.

I had no real inkling when I went to that doctor's appointment that I had stepped up to a precipice. I suppose we never really do. We cross a line and think nothing much has changed. Only later do we see that it was the first step in a long journey away from the righteous path.

After that first injection, I was soon well practiced in performing what was necessary for myself. I found that it was more palatable to inject myself in the buttock rather than just above the knee, which could be painful. I continued to do this for the next six years of my life.

The effects of the testosterone were immediate. The doctor was right in one sense: I did feel as though I were twenty-one again, not the least in my libido. After Lydia left and finding myself single once more, I started going out in New York City on the hunt for "true love" — but, of course, looking in all the wrong places.

It was just another way to try regaining some sense of adequacy after the failure of Misavi. Of course, promiscuity was doomed to fail on that score just as badly. I was trying to put the last three or four years behind me. But really, I was just digging myself farther down into the same hole. I had a new wingman: "Jersey" George, whom everyone knew only as "Jersey." He was a cousin of my other friend, Mark, and we hung out a lot at the time.

We would head into New York City and hit up every place we could in a single night — bars and clubs. Jersey worked in finance but hated his job. To be honest, I think he and I would meet up just so we could medicate ourselves together. After all, misery loves company. Living in the city, he knew all the best places. It was about the worst kind of environment in which you could put a man who had just started injecting himself with testosterone. I was like a lion on the prowl, never satisfied, never wanting to go home. Jersey sensed that I was different. He just didn't know why. No one did. It was my secret.

I had an insane amount of new confidence. It was all false confidence, but it had the desired effect, so I didn't really stop to question it. At the same time, I was going to gyms more, bodybuilding, sculpting my physique, manufacturing an idol out of my own body.

Now when I look back, I realize that there's a colossal irony to that fact. In the Bible, especially the Old Testament, the people of Israel are told again and again not to create false idols for themselves. Again and again, they go ahead and do it. Why the prohibition? Why is it a lie and a sin? Because human beings themselves are created to be the image-bearers of the one true God. *We can be idols.* That's why when we desecrate and abuse ourselves and each other, we are dishonoring the creator. We are blaspheming Him in the same way you would be if you were to spit on a cross.

The steroids were changing me, turning me into a muscle-bound "macho" man. And with the physicality of that image came the language too. I spoke differently. I talked tough. Me, a tough guy — the boy who couldn't say boo to a fly.

And it was all counterfeit. All just chemicals in my blood.

Sculpting a False Image

The next stage after the testosterone was an anabolic called Anavar. It came in the form of a little pill that is taken four a day for a period of about twelve weeks. One of the friends I met at the gym where I was going introduced me to it. His name was George. He was an amateur bodybuilder obsessed with his hero, Arnold Schwarzenegger. But he never really made it himself. George told me bodybuilders use Anavar for competitions. They "stack" it — that's the term. So, I started stacking.

Meanwhile, I was hitting the club scene hard. I had friends now who were promoters at a lot of different lounges and clubs. And now, despite having tried to warn Gabriella off it in the past, I started using cocaine myself. Funny how things change over time.

I mean, what a mess, right? I had a cocktail of anabolic steroids, synthetic testosterone, and now cocaine fizzing through my veins. I was around thirty-two or thirty-three at this time. And now life spiraled in a different direction. Anabolics were easy to come by once you knew how to get them, so suddenly I was dealing it too, selling vials of testosterone, mostly to other gym rats like myself. All of us were living in pursuit of an image, an amalgam of the images we saw on the covers of the bodybuilding magazines we were reading—the men we aspired to be.

I was being pulled completely away from the true image whom God had created me to be. Wrenched out of shape until I looked and felt like a warped sculpture, I was heading in a direction totally contradictory to the course I knew in my heart of hearts I should be headed, to the work that God, in His still, small voice, was calling me to. But I still wasn't listening. I needed to be woken up.

The Alarm Sounds

As for the consequences of the Misavi disaster, I was still making payments on that loan, but not big enough to erode the amount we owed. I was making all the interest payments, and that was okay — Manny had other things to deal with. Then after a while, Mom stepped in and started paying off the capital, which still amounted to something like $350,000. Unsurprisingly, this created the beginning of a wedge between us, as you would expect. Manny just didn't have the money, simple as that. I did what I could. But the reality was that mom was the one having to pay off the majority of that loan.

There would come a time when I would have to ask Mom's forgiveness for handing her this huge financial burden. But at that time, much as I told myself that I was doing all I could, the truth is that I was spending a lot of money on other things, still running full tilt after the things of the world.

I was entirely living life for myself. After all, I could see nothing outside of myself to live for. So, I filled myself up with whatever I could find — drugs, women, my own appearance. But as fast as I tried to fill myself up with these things, the next moment I would be feeling empty inside.

By around 2016 I had been in the bodybuilding game long enough to feel confident that I should be getting myself into some modelling on Instagram. Yeah, as silly as that sounds, this was another way to be in the spotlight and get noticed.

"'Ah,' the Preacher cries out: 'Vanity of vanities! All is vanity!'" (Ecclesiastes 1:2, author's paraphrase).

Yet this was what I was chasing — the ephemeral unreality of personal vanity. I was moving among people who were living the same lie: "the beautiful people," "the people of the mirror," you might say — all strong and confident on the surface, weak and ashamed underneath.

So, I was led into a relationship with the next woman in my life, an Ecuadorian model, as beautiful as she was toxic. She was literally a beauty pageant model. I was a gym rat. A match made in heaven, right? (or else the other place).

Her name was Lynn. It was she who introduced me to the pageant world, specifically a friend of hers named Jaime who was the director of Mr. Ecuador USA. By the time I met him, I had already been living with Lynn for six months, and we would have some barn-storming arguments. Boy, that girl knew how to rage! Mostly it was because she perceived some slight from me or thought I had shown some other woman undue attention. If I had, it was never intentional. After the first couple of fights, I knew better than to do that. She was always creating a massive scene, screaming at me in clubs or restaurants before storming out and charging through oncoming traffic. It was crazy behavior. She would play crazy games, like pretending to throw herself out of the car while it was moving fast to teach me a lesson. Probably all because she missed her calling as an actress, although that sort of behavior wasn't uncommon with Spanish women. That's a harsh generalization, perhaps, but it's true.

Even if it might be expected, I certainly had never experienced anything like this in my life. There was one incident that escalated and escalated to the point at which she called the cops on me. I just left the situation but still ended up having to go down to the precinct to make a statement. The whole scenario was absurd, arising out of absolutely nothing. It was bewildering being with her, and borderline abusive, especially when she was throwing stuff at me. These days I believe you would call it gaslighting, as she played with my mind, making me think I must be crazy.

That incident was a wake-up call. I got out of the relationship about a month later. I had hung around as other things started to come out of her — stories of the trauma of her past, abuse at the hands of her father, self-harm, and so on. It was full-on. I tried helping her by taking her to a psychologist, but she only seemed to get more angry and more volatile after that. Finally, I just had to quit. It was never real love in the first place.

Personal Prophets

Anyway, Lynn aside, she had also introduced me to a personal trainer who was helping Jaime with this Mr.

Ecuador USA pageant competition. His name was Marlon. Marlon was to play a key role in my life, as you'll see.

We had met at a gala event whose purpose was to help out in the Spanish community. He had his own backstory of bodybuilding and modelling, which had all gone down the tubes when he injured his back, so he had turned to becoming a trainer instead. Now he was suggesting that I should come and train with him, taking my fitness to the next level. He was younger than me, and yet in some ways he became something like a mentor to me.

Therefore, I started going to train at Marlon's home gym, which he had set up at the back of his parents' house. That was really where we started getting to know each other. And slowly, little by little, I started spilling the beans, opening up and finally speaking to somebody about how I was feeling, confiding in him. It felt good, because up until then I had had no one to genuinely confide in.

Marlon was to become a very good friend, maybe the best I've ever had. You'll see why I can say that a little further on.

Much of the way in which he helped came from the fact that he himself was being mentored by some wise and effective people. You see, Marlon and his wife, Stephanie, were involved in the Amway business, which proved to be instrumental in their lives. At first, he would often share business books and entrepreneurial wisdom he had picked up; but soon our friendship started encompassing more than that. It seems odd to say, but he was becoming like a brother to me, investing time and thought into my life. He cared about what happened to me, what I was doing with my life.

He saw *me*. Not the image of me that I was trying to present to the world but rather the actual me that lay beneath, the man who needed a friend.

It was Marlon who brought the word *God* back into my life, exemplifying what it was to be a follower of Christ. And while he never spoke to me in those terms for a long time, he described himself as "a vessel of God".

I would go one step further. I would call him a *spokesman* for God. That's what he was for me. And it was through him that I started sensing that God wasn't done with me yet.

In long, long stretches of the Old Testament the people of Israel had fallen away from their true covenant, their true calling. King after king after king after king were recorded as doing evil in the sight of the Lord. The reason: they chose to serve themselves and to serve the false idols of fertility gods or sex goddesses or gods of prosperity, even gods of death. They were lost, hopelessly lost. And yet God was not done with them either. He continued sending prophets, men and women whom He had appointed to speak for Him, to these high and mighty kings and their wayward people.

Sometimes the prophets were heeded; sometimes they were ignored. They brought with them warnings, yes, but they also brought promises — that God is always faithful, that He had made a covenant with His people, that He would never forsake His side of the bargain. His hand was always outstretched and open, ready to receive His children back, if only they would turn back. If only they would take His hand once more . . .

And through Marlon, God started weaving a different thread into my life.

Around the same time, someone else came into my life. Her name was Leslie, a Puerto Rican lady three years younger than me. She came into the store one day when I was slicing some deli meat for a club sandwich. Before long she was a regular customer. We would talk, first about nothing too heavy, but then she started introducing her faith into the conversation. God. Christianity. After that came books she thought I should read, mostly Christian books with a motivational angle by authors whom I would never go to now. But then . . . they certainly knew how to sugar-coat a message to make the whole idea of faith in God seem more plausible—more palatable—to someone as far fallen-away as I was. So, I would read them, telling myself they were a way of getting some good wisdom on how to push on in life without dealing with the faith aspect of them too directly. But I was willing to listen. My ears were slowly opening. The brand on the "packaging" wasn't off-putting to me, as it might be to many others.

It was only much later that Leslie told me she had walked into the store that first time only because she felt God prompt her to do so. She sensed there was something that needed to happen. It would take a long time before she found out what that something was.

In fact, Leslie had become a Christian only shortly before we met, prompted to explore the deeper meaning of life when her mother passed away from cancer. I guess you could say she was full of the fire of that new faith, that first love that burns so brightly.

There was never anything romantic between us. I was still "looking for my future wife" in all the wrong places.

But it was an enduring, thoughtful friendship that encouraged me toward study and reflection in a way nothing else had up until that point. She switched on a part of my brain that had lain dormant my whole life.

None of this really impacted how I was living my life yet. I was still going out a lot, still snorting cocaine, still up to my neck in anabolic drugs and that whole "gym rat" lifestyle. It was becoming more of a double life too. Clean cut and respectable at the store, a pillar of the community — well, maybe that's pushing it! Certainly, I was someone people knew and relied on but someone else entirely on a Saturday night in the city.

I remember taking a trip to Colombia around this time with my old buddy Saul. We went to the city of Medellin, essentially to hook up with women because we had heard that was what Medellin was good for. Saul was shocked that I was even doing drugs at this age, since it felt a long time ago that we had been messing with that stuff together. We didn't fall out or anything, but he certainly made it clear that he didn't approve, and he saw me in a different light after that, a little shady. It was a glimpse in the mirror for me, a sliver of truth of what I had become behind the façade, behind the mask — and the beard I had grown at the time. I suppose I had convinced myself that this was me growing up, a mature man making it in the world. Saul made me feel as if it were all an act.

He was closer to the truth.

It made me question: *Who have I become? Which of these two lives I'm living is closer to the real me? The stand-up guy who helps run the deli store, whom folks have seen grow up from a little boy? Mikey, who used to run that smart up-and-coming restaurant, who*

*enjoys a drink now and then? Or the man doing coke at the weekends
and selling anabolic drugs on the side? Mikey the hustler?*

The truth is that both were masks, images created to
serve a purpose, that purpose being to hide me from the
world. That said, very few people knew about Mikey the
hustler. I made sure of that. I think there was still some
instinct within me, some faint voice of conscience that was
calling me back.

Back to the light.

But there was that shadow too, the serpent in the grass
that didn't want me to return, that wanted to hold me in the
darkness with him forever.

Everything I Ever Wanted

When I came back from Colombia, I started training hard.
For the next four months straight, I was in the gym two
hours a day, seven days a week in preparation for this new
pageant competition, I had stopped doing everything
harmful for a time, including the drinking. That alone made
me feel a whole lot better.

In the meantime, Jaime, the event director to whom
Lynn had introduced me, had been busy talking up this first
ever "Mr. Ecuador USA" contest, which was to be held in
the New York and New Jersey area. It was to include
contestants from all over the country and from Ecuador as
well. In fact, most of them that first year did come from
Ecuador. The only stipulation was that both contestant's
parents were Ecuadorian. The whole thing was funded by
the New Jersey Ecuadorian Committee, so there was a real
local community vibe to the entire setup.

So, the day came around: June 30, 2017. All the contestants are there at the Fiesta Banquet Hall in Woodridge, New Jersey, prepping for the competition, fourteen of us in total. While Jaime and his team were setting up the stage and sound system, laying out the tables and chairs, finalizing the promotions, and briefing the guest judges, we ran through our rehearsals, going through the program order, figuring out our markers as to where we were supposed to be and when, running through the questions we would be asked—all the while, sizing up the opposition. It was clear who was the favorite: a Ken doll look-alike from Ecuador who was about six-foot-two with classic Latino good looks, chiseled jaw, the whole nine yards. The dope was that he had come from Ecuador specifically to win the prize. Back there he was a successful model. Everyone expected him to win. So did I. After all, his name was Fabrizio. He was born for this.

The stage was set up in a T-formation. There would be two hosts — one male, one female. The evening was going to run with everything in Spanish, including the answers to all questions. My Spanish wasn't as good then as it is now, so already I was a little daunted. I had been practicing with Marlon and his wife, Stephanie, who would often prep both guys and girls for these kinds of pageant contests (they were and are still an awesome team!). Despite it all, I was resigned to the fact that there was no chance of my winning this competition without fluent Spanish.

There were to be different rounds so that each of us would appear in three different costumes or "looks": lounge suit, beachwear, tuxedo. Hence the need to have worked out for the previous six months: people were going to be seeing me half-naked. It goes without saying that I was slathered head to toe in fake tan, hair freshly cut, beard trimmed, and ready to go. But I was in good shape too. I looked sharp — as did all the others, I must admit.

I was contestant number seven.

We were all called out, one by one, and soon I was up. So off I went, up and down the length of the runway. To be honest, I never felt more like a piece of meat in my whole life. You can imagine. The cheers, the spotlights, the music, the MC cracking jokes. I had never seen anything like it. I worked it as best I could, and then before I knew it, I was backstage again.

By the second round everyone had their favorites and the cheers got even louder. I remember the two tables of audience members nearest the stage were clearly plants, all of them cheering for Fabrizio, the six-foot Ken doll. It had never occurred to me to bring my own team of cheerleaders. It was all a bit bewildering, to be honest.

Backstage, everyone was nervous, so someone had the bright idea of a little Dutch courage. Before long we were all getting a little loose on champagne that someone else was paying for (Hey—why not?). It had the desired effect. I started to relax and feel more confident. After the final tuxedo round, I was feeling relieved but also having a good time now, waiting with everyone else for the team of judges to come out to announce the winner.

"Ladies and gentlemen, after counting the scores, I have to tell you that it is extremely close. In fact, so close that . . .

we have ourselves a tie between Fabrizio and Michael." Cue extreme volumes of cheering (especially from tables one and two). I was stunned, but also stoked, the voice in my head—or the alcohol in my veins—yelling, "You're the man!" After all, Fabrizio was twenty-three. I was thirty-six.

Compared to him, I was practically an old man.

"What happens now?" I asked one of the judges over the commotion.

"We give you each a question blind. No prep, just off the cuff."

With my poor Spanish I was sure this would be my downfall — until Marlon slid up to me and told me he had heard through the grapevine what the question would be. "I'm only telling you because of your Spanish, right?"

"Just tell me," I said, pressing him.

"All right, all right." He leaned closer and dropped his voice. "They're going to ask what you'd do for the community if you won the title." He pulled back and slapped me on the shoulder. "You've got one minute to think about it, buddy, 'cause you're going in cold."

A few seconds later Fabrizio was called out onto the stage. He seemed very confident. The girls around the front two tables were chanting his name. The question was asked, and at first, he was doing well, but just at the tables full of girls start chanting his name. He started blathering on about how he was so good-looking and that he could do this and that. He talked on and on, but all that was coming across was how conceited he was. You could literally feel the crowd slipping away from him. It was kind of magical, a gift handed to me because now it was so obvious what I needed to do. And by the time he was walking off stage and I was called on, the crowd had gone completely silent.

I stepped forward up to the mic and felt the light shining on my face. Below me the audience was a blur, and not just from the alcohol.

I told myself, *Just be yourself. Be genuine. Be authentic. For once in your life, Mikey.*

"So, Michael, if you were to win tonight's contest and be crowned Mr. Ecuador USA, what would you do for the community?"

I started talking. The voice that came out was all choked up with nerves. My heart was pumping fast. "First of all, I would dedicate that honor to the memory of my father, who died of cancer nineteen years ago." I worried it sounded contrived, even though it had come straight from my heart.

The crowd released a huge collective sigh of empathy at that. You could feel their emotions practically vibrating the glassware on the tables. It was a while before I could continue in my halting Spanish.

"Ultimately, it's my belief that to win this competition, a man must be humble. He must be respectful of those around him. He must carry himself in a certain way so that when people look at him, they see his humility. That is the quality I would bring to the community."

I paused, thinking of what to say next. But already the host had whipped the microphone away, and that was that. Apparently, that was enough from me. Instead, the MC seized hold of Fabrizio and me and dragged us both to the front of the stage, two perfectly groomed grinning man-dolls on display before the whooping crowd.

"And the winner is" — I glanced down at my family and friends, barely enough of them to fill a table — "Michael Cabezas!"

I couldn't believe it. I had won. The crowd nearly yelled the roof off the building. I had won. I didn't think I had ever felt so stunned. I had no words. The cameras flashed, the music cranked up, the cheering resounded. I felt like a rockstar, like a somebody, right? Someone to look at. Someone to notice. At last.

Pride before a Fall

Truly I wished my father could have seen me then.

Next thing, I found myself swept along in the flood of a strange and sudden feeling that this was what I had been hunting for my whole life, a moment when people would sit up, look at me, applaud me, and say, "Yeah, kid. Look at you. You've done all right."

I had no idea I could win anything like that. I had had no expectation to. And yet suddenly there I was, being crowned

"Mr. Ecuador USA".

The pageant king.

After they had handed out the awards, that's when the real drinking started. People wanted to come up and shake my hand and offer their congratulations. Everyone wanted a toast with me. Champagne and cocktails were flowing like a river. The night started feeling loose, and me with it. Thank God, I had someone watching out for me. I don't say that flippantly either. At a certain point in the evening a friend from the contest named Francisco came up to me and told me to give him my keys.

"What?"

"Your car keys. Come on, buddy. You aren't driving anywhere tonight. It's been a big night for you. I'll drive you home whenever you're ready."

I hadn't even thought about what was coming next. So almost without a word, I handed over my keys, meek as a lamb — not something I had ever done before. The fact that it was Francisco was random. He had come over from Ecuador to compete. Sure, we were on friendly terms, but he was hardly someone I could expect to have my back. Maybe later, but not then.

The next thing I remember is walking out of the banqueting hall with a bunch of friends. Francisco was there. Several of us piled into my car. Far too many of us, in fact. I think we were seven in a white BMW X4 M — a compact SUV designed to seat five. Francisco still had my keys, so he was driving. He had already told me that he was a Christian and he didn't drink.

We were headed to an after-party in another club in their Ironbound district.

So, in the front we had Francisco driving and Jaime, the director of the show, in the passenger seat. In the back there were two girls, Lilly and Nadine, two contestants (men), and finally me. Seven in all. I was last in, so I found myself wedged awkwardly on one of the guys' laps on the right side next to the door.

We headed south on Route 21, just reaching that part of town where there were streetlights as we drove on into the city. Two of the guys were chatting in the middle of the car while I was talking to Nadine on my left. She was getting married soon and was showing me her engagement ring. I remember saying, "Wow! That's a beautiful diamond —"

The next thing I knew, I was hanging half out of the car door. The door itself was completely ripped off the car.

The impact came between those two moments. I was knocked unconscious in an instant. When I came to, the two girls were nowhere to be seen—they had been thrown completely clear. All the men who were strapped into the car were yelling in confusion and shock, obviously in major distress.

Immediately I felt my head and my knee hurting as well as I was slumped out of the door. Only then did the thought form in my head that we had been in an accident. I rolled over and found, thank God, that I was able to get up. I could see Nadine. But there was no sign of Lilly at all. There was a lot of smoke. I saw that we were now on the northbound side of Route 21, my car having slewed across the highway into the other lanes of traffic. There were several vehicles involved. I had no idea exactly what had happened.

And then there was Marlon. He came out of nowhere, directing me to do something, but I was still so dazed and confused that I couldn't understand what he was saying.

"What are you doing here?" I asked, words slow and labored. I knew he and his wife had left to go home, which was in the opposite direction from the banqueting hall. But he didn't answer my question, just pointed urgently at another body on the tarmac. It was Lilly, lying unconscious a few feet from me. I picked myself up and we went to her, stumbling over my feet. She was coming around but barely able to stand. As Marlon and I hefted her up and helped her to the sidewalk, my senses started coming back to me.

I repeated my question to Marlon: "What are you doing here?" Don't get me wrong, I was extremely glad that he was.

"I'll explain later," he said, still more concerned for the two girls.

It was only once the ambulance had arrived and we had all been transported to the hospital that he answered my question. The girls were in a bad way, they had taken some serious knocks, but at least they were in good hands now.

"Well?" I persisted. "I thought you guys were going home."

"We were," Marlon replied. "I mean, we weren't going to come with you. But then . . ."

"Then what?"

He looked at me and clasped my hand. "But then God told us to follow you."

He must have seen the shock on my face, the incomprehension. "Come on," he said gently. "It's been a big night for you. I'll run you home."

CHAPTER SEVEN

Time to Turn

As many have learned and later taught, you don't realize Jesus is all you need until Jesus is all you have. - Tim Keller

The time of impact was 1:15 a.m. on Saturday July 1, 2017.

At precisely the same time in another part of the city, my friend Leslie was woken up from her sleep. *Pray for Michael. Pray for his protection.* That's what she heard — so she told me later after she learned about the accident on social media. So, pray is what she did.

The police arrived at the scene at 1:18 a.m. It was a mess. There were three vehicles involved. My car had been the first one that the car that had lost control hit.

At the very moment of impact, Leslie was sitting up in bed praying for my protection, for my "safety and security." She had no clue as to why she had been woken up; this had never happened to her before. At that stage we were not particularly close friends, hardly more than acquaintances.

It takes some explaining for that.

My own belief is that God had just spared my life, saved me from either death or serious injury. My BMW was totaled. Both girls had been thrown out of the car. Marlon had peeled them both off the tarmac and carried them to the sidewalk out of further harm's way. Two ambulances came and we were taken, along with several other injured people, to the hospital, where we were given a series of MRIs scans and X-rays. Amazingly, none of us had life-threatening injuries, although the girls were more cut up than me. Both had to be held in intensive care for some time.

Marlon had described what he saw from his vantage point following behind us in his car. He told me later that he had no intention to trail us after the party in Newark was winding down. As I described, the only explanation he offered for why he did was that God had told him to. He never elaborated on how exactly and I never asked. But as I thought back over the evening's events, the less sense it made to me that I had walked away from that accident unscathed. A near-death encounter like that gets you thinking. But when Leslie told me her piece of the puzzle—the only rational conclusion, it seemed to me, was that there was indeed something real to this God whom she wanted to tell me about.

I remember sitting on the edge of my bed with the thought in my head: *I think God just saved my life.*

People ask for signs. Well, as far as I was concerned, here was an alarm bell going off loud and clear. There *is* a God—a God who saves, a God who wanted to save *me*. But why? What purpose did He have for my life that made it worth saving?

I didn't know the answer to that question.

But I wanted to find out.

Here is the deep irony, though. That mindset lasted for about a day before it slipped away again.

When the kings of Israel in the Old Testament reverted again and again into their idolatry and unbelief, even after prophet after prophet appeared to remind them of the truth, what was it that made them fall away? Forgetfulness? Ingratitude? Self-will? A determination that they always knew better?

No doubt, all those things played their part. I think it's the same for us. The signs are all around us, even within us through the promptings of our conscience, however callous that conscience may have become. We take the point one minute and then forget it the very next.

So, was I grateful that God had spared me? Consciously, not very. Instead, I was left with the physical and mental fallout of the accident. My shoulder was torn. My knee was badly swollen. My mind was foggy for weeks afterwards, probably from having been knocked out cold for a few seconds.

I found out more details in the days afterwards. The left door had been ripped clean off when the impact occurred. The driver who hit us had been drunk and fled the accident. No one saw him leave at the time. But he wasn't exactly smart. He could be identified from his car, of course, and from his wallet, which he left behind. That didn't stop him from reporting the car stolen two days later in a pretty weak attempt to cover his tracks. Still, the law eventually caught up with him, but all they could pin him for was responsibility for the accident and fleeing the scene of the accident. He lost his license and had to pay a fine, but he was never charged with DWI (driving while intoxicated) because under New Jersey law he would have needed to be tested that night.

But the legal tangle of all that meant that Lilly and Nadine in fact had to sue my insurers to cover their injuries. Francisco, as the driver of my car, was held in no way culpable.

He and I met up a few days later for a cup of coffee. He told me again how he felt prompted to take my keys off me because he could see how inebriated I was getting at the show. And we both reflected how fortunate it was that I wasn't driving. Had I been, with that level of alcohol in my blood, they would have thrown the book at me. He explained that at the very last moment before impact he had just managed to swerve to the right so that the other car hit us obliquely down the left side. If his reactions had been any slower and it had been a head-on collision . . . forget about it.

So, there were all the pieces in place to mitigate what could have been a horrific tragedy: Francisco driving, senses still sharp so he could swerve at the last moment; Marlon right there behind us to snatch Nadine off the road almost immediately — otherwise she could easily have been hit by other vehicle as she lay there injured. There was Leslie, praying for my protection. Put all of it together, and it feels like a moment when the serpent, the enemy of my soul, wanted to take me out. But God had already countered it.

There was one other interesting thing about the aftermath of the accident.

After we met for coffee, Francisco literally disappeared.

I never saw him again, never heard from him again. I tried to contact him, but he never responded to my texts. I have two explanations. First, because he had been driving, he wanted nothing to do with the legal process that followed. Although he had lived in the United States before, he had returned to Ecuador by then. He was visiting the United States at that time only for the competition, so probably he went back to Ecuador to carry on with his life. But that doesn't explain why he would cut all communication with me.

The other explanation may sound a little "out there." That Francisco was an angel.

The letter to the Hebrews in the New Testament says of angels, "Are they not all ministering spirits sent out to serve for the sake of those who are to inherit salvation?" (Hebrews 1:14).

As you will see, this explanation fits the facts a good deal more closely.

Happily, I was equally well defended in the material world as in the spiritual realm when it came to the legal fallout of the accident. My lawyer, Steven, who remains a friend, did a great job of taking care of all the claims and counterclaims flying around.

But really, it was from this point onward that I became conscious of God wooing me back to Him with His grace, back into His arms.

Eventually my injuries healed up, although my shoulder would continue giving me some trouble for a while to come. Part of the follow-up to my victory as "Mr. Ecuador USA" was to participate in a charity pageant back in the old country, as it were — Ecuador. In fact, I was all set to judge the event, to be held in the city of Ambato in February 2018, but for various reasons I initiated plans for another trip sooner than that, in November 2017, only a few months after all these more dramatic incidents. The motivation for that first trip was something that's hard to explain. It just felt like a compulsion, something I needed to do.

The closer that my departure drew in time, the stronger came the sense that something was waiting for me there in Ecuador, that there was some purpose to my going. I didn't know where this feeling was coming from. But it had prompted me to fall in alongside Jaime, the Mr. Ecuador USA director, who was coordinating a charity event there for orphan kids and the elderly.

The community we were aiming to help were desperately poor and lived in one big home in the city of Cuenca. Jaime had arranged for us to bring them supplies of everyday items—pens and paper, for example, for their schooling—as well as more basic needs like food.

The last time I had been in Ecuador I was seven years old. But this time, when I witnessed the poverty all around me, it hit me in a different way. I can't explain it. Of course, I had seen poverty in the United States. I had seen it all over. But now I was seeing it with different eyes. New eyes.

I guess having won this competition, I *was* Mr. Ecuador USA to a lot of the people I was meeting. I came with a label, so to speak, and so in that guise people wanted to meet me and get to know me. They looked up to me. For my part, when I was doing this charity work, moving among some of the poorest of the poor in Ecuador, I was struck by the kids. They were humble, but they also carried a certain dignity. It's as if their humility had the capacity to expand their personal presence, and yet I find it hard to adequately describe what I mean by that. It was almost as if with all the usual masks and facades of the world that people wear stripped away from them, you were able to see more clearly the image of God in them, the image of their creator. And somehow this made them greater, not lesser, than other more affluent people.

I was so touched by them that when I returned to the United States, I started looking into how to start up my own nonprofit organization for kids. I spoke to a couple of people who had done it, trying to figure out what it would take.

During this whole time, I had been courting a certain stunning lady named Claudia. She was only twenty-two years old so there was quite an age gap — I was thirty -six at the time. She had won the sister competition to mine, "Miss Ecuador New Jersey." Quite the perfect match, huh? Not exactly, it turned out. However, for most of the second half of 2017 I was pursuing her, trying to win her interest, mainly through buying her expensive gifts. The first was a trip to Cancún, Mexico. How's that for a first date? It was a classic case of trying to buy a woman's love. And eventually, in December of that year, we started dating properly so that by early 2018 I considered us a couple (though I would soon dispel of this notion).

The official follow-up trip after the two pageant competitions that had been held in the United States was planned for February 2018. The New Jersey Ecuadorian Committee had subsidized around fifteen people, including the winner and runner-up of each competition, to travel to Ecuador for the Festival of Fruit and Flowers ("La Fiesta de la Fruta y Las Flores") in the city of Ambato. It is late summer in that month and a beautiful time to visit. The festival is a pretty big deal there, part of it a huge parade through the streets of Ambato.

As we traveled there, I had built the trip up in my mind as a great coming-together of all I believed I wanted — weaving together my people, my heritage, some recognition and acclaim for the hard work I had put into my appearance. This awakened a desire in me to reach outward and help others, and of course this beautiful young woman whom I desired and had pursued for many months.

It was all going to be perfect.

Except that it wasn't.

Right from the start Claudia acted distant from me, not really wanting to associate with me. I felt rejected. I *was* rejected. And since I had waited and hoped for a long time for this relationship to take off, the fact that it was already stalling was painful to me.

Maybe it was that disappointment that redirected my focus more onto the poverty that I was witnessing. There were more charity visits arranged. But also, I was just walking the streets, seeing the poor around the area, especially the kids. And it really started to press deeply into my heart.

There was one moment that struck me, during the parade itself in Ambato. I was walking along with the rest of the parade. There was the loud music and the bright colors of all the floats and banners, various cohorts of kids from different schools marching down the historic streets, flowers and fruit everywhere. The crowds were lining the streets on the other side of the guardrails that mark our route, cheering us on as we walked by. I felt great. I felt like somebody. The warm, elusive feeling was captured in my hands for once. People keep calling me over to the guardrails, wanting to shake my hand and take my picture, sometimes with them, sometimes by myself.

A small child and his parents called me over. There was a little boy with them, their son, a child so small that his head didn't even come up to the rail. But he called to me so loudly that I went over. He held his arms out to me, a look of pure excitement on his face. Without really thinking, I just scooped him up and over the rail and held him in my arms. He was as light as a little bird, his eyes bright and alive. An official photographer was walking along behind us in the parade, and we turned to have our picture taken. This little kid was just beaming up at me, as if I were some superstar, as if I were really somebody.

And it suddenly hit me: *I'm no one special. Why is he looking at me like that? I'm nobody. What am I doing here? This kid has more humility, more love, more joy in him than I do.* And looking down into his face, I realized that I was envious of him. Here was I, who had grown up in the United States with all the good things I had taken for granted, all these advantages, and this kid had nothing. He was looking up at me as if I were his hero. And yet I was the one envious of him. He had something that I did not.

I can't say exactly what it was that he had. Maybe it was his innocence, that radiant innocence in his face that I lost so many years before — a goodness, a sweetness. And I suddenly feel the inversion of the whole scene. *I* should have been applauding *him*; *I* should have been idolizing *him*. All this around me, this parade, was fake, a mere illusion. But he had something real.

The boy was only five or six years old, yet in his face for a moment I glimpsed myself, that six-year-old kid who had had that same goodness in him. And somehow in the thirty years since, I had squandered it in pursuit of all the wrong things in the hunger to create this succession of false images for myself — and none of them could replicate what I really wanted, who I really was . . .

That reality felt so far away in that moment. I thought maybe that kid (me) was lost forever.

Falsehood. Lies. That was the life I was living. That was the path I had chosen. I knew then that I needed to find a different path — not a path forward but one I could find by turning around and walking backwards, to retrace my steps, to find once more the true path that I had strayed from a long time ago.

Here I was, the big success. Michael Cabezas—Mr. Ecuador USA. A pageant king. Yet I knew it was a lie. I had conformed to the lie of the world.

This was not success. The pageant king must die.

The little boy in me must live again.

It was just a moment, a lightning flash in which for an instant I saw the reality of the life I was living with piercing clarity. Here I was, at the top of the mountain, everyone around cheering me on, calling my name, applauding me. And yet I felt utterly hollow inside.

It's as someone once said: What they never tell you while you're scaling that mountain is that when you reach the top, there's nothing there. So, if the mountain I was climbing only led to a great void of emptiness, where was the real substance to be found?

Something else was happening as I looked at this kid: my heart was softening. And perhaps that was the beginning of the answer to my question, compassion awakened in a hard, hard heart that had been positioned only inward toward my wants and needs. Maybe at last it could slowly turn my gaze outward.

Even heavenward.

Even when I had fallen for this succession of beautiful women, when I was loving them, still it was about me. It was about how they served my image. It was about loving myself, not them for who they truly were. I wanted them to fill the bottomless hole in me, something they couldn't possibly achieve. That's not love. That's codependence.

Augustine wrote, "You have made us for yourself, O Lord, and our hearts are restless until they rest in You." I was about to discover the truth of this for myself.

That outward love was born in that encounter. A divine spark of grace.

Changing Course

The contrast between how this trip affected me and how it affected Claudia could not have been greater. While I felt humbled, she became distant. She seemed to think she was better than everything and everyone around her. I can't blame her for that. I'm sure I would have felt the same at a different stage in my life. But the result was to push us even farther apart. She hid away with the family she had over there. She didn't want to hang out with the rest of us from the visiting committee. She instead went to stay with the family she had there. The fact that this meant turning her back on me as well bothered me. I took it very personally; I'm not going to lie. I still wanted her love, and I wasn't getting it.

And still there was this push-and-pull factor between returning to the "righteous path," if I can call it that, and continuing the way I was headed.

I had resolved to set up a nonprofit organization when I returned to the United States to raise funds and support for the poor and needy in Ecuador. But instead, all my energy and headspace were going into trying to win the heart of this young girl. As noted earlier, in March of that year I surprised her with a trip to Mexico. This seemed to work for a short space of time. She became more interested but obviously for the wrong reasons: I was spending a lot of money on her. Of course, I was projecting too much onto her. She was only twenty-two and wasn't ready for what I wanted. Besides, what I wanted was not at all what I needed. Slowly, inch by inch, I was figuring that out for myself.

Even though I had caught a glimpse of the true path I needed to follow, that whole period was one of turmoil for me. I won another award, this time as "Latin Model of the Year" in the borough of Queens, New York. I had done nothing to earn this. The powers that be simply voted and

I was declared the winner. It was ironic that just as I was starting to glimpse the emptiness of it all, I had never been so popular, never won such acclaim, nor so effortlessly.

As British author C. S. Lewis wrote to a friend who was drawing closer to finding faith, "The enemy will not see you vanish into God's company without an effort to reclaim you."

It was obvious as to where my weak spots lay pride, vanity, the nearly insatiable thirst for attention and affirmation, all of it stemming, no doubt, from my father's neglect, his inability to say to me, *there you are. I see you.*

But there is another father who is able. More than able. The professional attention I was getting was a distraction from Him. Even though my folks had done their best to cultivate humility in me, my ego was being inflated beyond anything I had ever experienced. I was starting to get decent traction in the world of semi-professional modelling, and of course any modest success was a lure to aim at greater things.

I was still running the business in the deli store, but my aspirations all lay in the glamor of the world of modelling and fitness. Every week there was another photo shoot. Every week I had hundreds of pictures taken of me, some paid, some unpaid. But all of it amounted to more media exposure and face recognition within the Ecuadorian community around New Jersey, or else headshots sent out to casting calls in New York City.

I'll have to admit that I loved it. It was my taste of the high life. I had rented a luxury apartment overlooking the Hudson River and the Manhattan skyline because that's what I thought a man living that kind of lifestyle ought to

do. I leased out my dream SUV, a 2018 BMW X5 Msport.
A lot of my life was on credit. So, it was unreal in that sense,
and unsustainable in the long term too.

Meanwhile, I took Claudia away to Dubai in an over-
the-top effort to win her heart. It was a fruitless endeavor,
as I should have realized long before. Even I was starting
to recognize that it wasn't love that I felt for her; I simply
wanted her as my trophy. I wanted her beauty, her success,
her popularity. I wanted her for how she would make me
look having her by my side. I guess I wouldn't be the first
man to want that, which doesn't make it any more
honorable.

By the end of this period, I had gotten myself into a big
financial hole, having racked up well over $100,000 in credit
card debt, all of it to maintain this carefully curated image,
the fulfilment of all that I thought I wanted to be, which
had kind of landed in my lap.

All through that year of 2018 I was becoming more and
more reliant on painkillers too. After the accident, I had
surgery on my shoulder, which hadn't been entirely
successful, so I started taking painkillers more regularly.
Regularity became more like reliance, all of this
supplemented by alcohol and from time-to-time cocaine
use as well.

I had a lot of crutches to remove.

Take any of those away and I would feel irritable, edgy,
and angry. So, I just kept on doing them, along with the
bodybuilding steroids — let's not forget them. Oh, my
blood must have been a real cocktail of chemicals by that
point!

Perhaps it was that which prompted my final lapse of judgment in my relationship with Claudia. I leased out another BMW for her in my name and on my insurance, because I had a better credit rating than she did. But I didn't like the independence this gave her. The problem underlying everything was that I wanted control over her. I grew possessive. We argued more and more. I started drinking more to forget about this hole I had dug myself into. With the booze and the combination of drugs in my system, my temper grew worse. And usually, I don't have a bad temper. But the arguments would grow more intense until one or the other of us would have to leave. If it was her, I wouldn't hear from her for the next couple of days.

The sooner the relationship came to its conclusion the better, and we finally parted company in August 2018. There was some dispute thanks to our entanglement surrounding her car. She refused to give it up even though there was no way she could keep up the payments and the insurance on her own. So, I ended up having to swipe it from under her nose using the spare fob key. I'm not proud of it. It was a messed-up situation and a messy way to end a relationship. But by then I was at the breaking point.

I had to take over the leasing arrangement with the car and find someone else to lease it to. That was a headache, and then someone scratched the paint just days before someone was due to view it. So, suddenly I was chasing around like a cat with its tail on fire, trying to get the paintwork fixed before the viewing. Thankfully, the car was ready, and the guy took it. But I remember thinking, *look at the chaos you've created for yourself, pursuing the wrong things.*

Things I knew to be wrong for me.

It was crazy, but very clear.

By the end of 2018 everything seemed to be building to a climax. Then in November I got a small contract as a model for an event in New York City showcasing a Russian jewelry brand. The woman who owned the company was a very glamorous lady of fifty or so, stunning to look at but a total seductress, danger rising off her like perfume — a true femme fatale. I remember the way she looked at me as though I were a morsel of meat, just another of "her models," as if she could pick up any one of us as if we were canapés on a serving dish.

It was funny. I had the clear sense that if I succumbed to her voluptuous charms, she would destroy me. And yet I would be there working, and she would throw that look at me, and that tug of war would start up again in my heart. Part of me would say, "I don't want to do this anymore: the women, the drugs, the money." It all started to look like a big inescapable sinkhole into which I was constantly being pulled back, even though I knew it wasn't good for me. And then the other part of me… looking at her as she looked at me.

Of course, I failed the test.

Again, I went against my instinct. Again, I succumbed to the temptation, to the stronger force, at least in the moment, even though I knew it was wrong.

The serpent in the grass, remember?

I see you, Michael. I see you too.

Her name was Katrina. The name of her company was "Devil's Tear." The main motif was a snake wrapped around a person's wrist.

The Bible says that the devil appears as an angel of light, deceiving us, luring us to himself with his lies. But sometimes he makes no pretense whatsoever. Sometimes you're staring right into the darkness, and you know it. Yet you go right ahead, marching on into it anyway.

Russian novelist Fyodor Dostoevsky wrote, "The awful thing is that beauty is mysterious as well as terrible. God and the devil are fighting there, and the battlefield is the heart of man."

Truly, there was a battle raging between good and evil. And the prize was my soul. There's a battle raging over all of us — over you, over me. The only thing is that some of us don't know it.

But I was blessed that my friend Marlon was fighting for good.

With the end of my relationship with Claudia, I became distraught, even though its demise was inevitable. I felt myself nose-diving into another depression. Thank God, Marlon was there to speak into my life.

I was still training with him regularly. He was a great listener, making it very easy for me to open to him about all I was feeling. I remember sitting down with him in a restaurant in Edgewater, New Jersey on a Sunday night. We were out with maybe ten other people, mostly from the Ecuadorian community. After a couple of drinks, I wasn't really into it anymore and was getting ready to leave, near the door, when it happened that Marlon and I had a moment alone. He looked me straight in the eye and asked, "What's wrong? I can see something's wrong, Mike. Tell me how you're really feeling."

No one else had ever spoken to me like that. So for once in my life, I was honest. And the next thing I know is it's all pouring out of me. I broke down, tears welling up, spilling down my face, while I tried finding the words for how unhappy I was, how lost I felt.

"I don't know what I'm doing. I just don't know what I'm doing with my life,'" I kept repeating, sobbing my heart out now.

"Hey, Mike." He put his hand on my shoulder. "Let me pray for you, man. D'you mind?"

Up till that point he had never asked to do that. But right then it seemed like the only thing he could say. I can't remember exactly what words he used. I remember fresh waves of tears poured out of me, though. And now they felt more like relief. I felt that God was reaching out to me through my friend Marlon. God was softening my heart, letting me know He was there, that He knew me, that He cared about me and my life. It was only a glimmer, as when you know someone is standing behind you, above you, but you haven't looked right at him or her face to face yet.

At the end of that conversation Marlon told me that he and his wife would go to a meetup on Sundays at a place on 34th Street in New York City. "A lot of good people," he said. "Would you come along with us?"

As the late Timothy Keller puts it, "If you want God's grace, all you need is need. All you need is nothing."

Nothing was all I had. "Sure," I said. "I'll come."

This is the place where I would surrender my life to Jesus Christ, my Lord and my Savior.

CHAPTER EIGHT

Love Sees

It is God's will through His wonderful grace that the prayers of His saints should be one of the great principal means of carrying on the designs of Christ's kingdom in the world. - Jonathan Edwards

Standing in line outside the building that used to be the Hammerstein Ballroom on 34th Street, I was amazed. It felt as though we were going into a concert. The people in the line were young and full of life and excitement with laughter and conversation, a levity in the air. The place was buzzing with expectation. And perhaps no one was feeling a greater sense of expectation than me.

Marlon had told me that a lot of people go to this meeting. "Good people," he called them. And certainly, if you caught anyone's eye, there was a smile never far from the surface. That seemed different, a little weird to be honest. But I was willing to be there — glad to be there — so I just moved on in with the rest of them. It was still New York, of course, so everyone had to pass through a security check to make sure no weapons were being carried in. Beyond that, attendants on the door were there to welcome us as we passed by. It felt like another world, an alien world.

Perhaps Marlon could sense this feeling in me. "Let me know what you think at the end. Meanwhile, just take it in, buddy." I looked around the atrium and noticed a big banner hanging above the doors leading into the auditorium. "Welcome Home," it said. I got the strangest feeling that those words were there just for me, as though I belonged there.

Marlon had left it all vague as to what I should expect. So, I looked around me, wondering who all these people were, absorbing all that I was seeing.

We made our way up to one of the upper galleries looking down onto the stage, and it felt as though we were at a music concert. We found seats in the row right at the back. I couldn't believe how many people there were filling up this place, seemingly hundreds of young people of every ethnicity under the sun. I had never been among a crowd of young people this big and felt a collective energy quite like this. It felt exciting and somehow good, a spirit of lightness, even joy.

"You Are Valued"

What I remember of that first experience was the speaker who stood up on stage and delivered his message. He turned out to be a well-known pastor at the time, famous across the nation, although as far as I was concerned, he was just a speaker on the platform. At that moment I didn't know him from Adam. But when he started speaking, it was as if he knew *me* inside out. His words were exactly what I needed to hear, his message fitting into the pain of my heart like a key in a lock. I listened, ears riveted to each syllable as he told me that I had to value myself, and of the damage that came from holding ourselves in low esteem. He described how easy it is to come up with a value for ourselves based on the wrong things: the amount of money we earn, the person we walk into a room with on our arm, the car we drive, the popularity we have among our friends, the reputation we have out in the world — and these days how many friends we have on social media and how many "likes" we get for our latest post. All that stuff, he said, is no basis on which to find your own value.

That's not how God sees you, he said. To God, your Father in heaven, you are infinitely valued *just for being who you are.* Just for existing, for being a man or a woman, a girl or a boy, one of His creatures who is made in His image. It doesn't matter what you've done or haven't done, what you're going to do. Nothing you've done or will do could make God value you any less or any more. He holds you in the highest esteem already. Indeed, He puts such a high value on you that He esteemed you worth dying for on a bloody cross so that you could be with Him forever, that He could know you and you know Him in an eternal relationship of love that has no end. That's how highly He values you, this preacher said.

The words fused together in my mind and then my heart. This "Father-God" values me? He died for me? He loves me? It seemed far more than I could dare to believe and an infinite distance from the value I put on myself. And for the first time I began to see. Who am I to say what I'm really worth? Did I know better than God? Didn't God have the final word on everything? Then who am I to deny the value that He puts on me, the value He then proved by His death on the cross for me, for all of us. You don't die for someone you care nothing about. You don't die for someone who's not worth something.

I walked away from that meeting with a new thought in my head. *Okay, God. You've got my attention.* I knew that message was meant for me, and now I was listening. My ears were open. I wanted to hear more.

When we got outside, I turned to Marlon.

"So . . . you're a Christian."

He nodded and smiled.

"Why didn't you tell me?"

"Did I need to?"

I shook my head. "I guess not." "How did you find it?" Marlon asked.

For a moment I couldn't find the words. There was too much going on inside. But at last, I spoke. "That was exactly what I needed to hear."

"Good. Then maybe you'll come again?" "Yeah." I chuckled. "Maybe I will."

And I did — nearly every Sunday, whenever I could. Even as I was still falling into the snares of the enemy, tumbling into a torrid and short-lived affair with the Russian jewelry diva, I kept on going to this church.

But to paraphrase C. S. Lewis again, it didn't matter. I was already in the meshes of the net. The Holy Spirit was after me, and as Lewis wrote as a comfort to his friend, "I doubt you'll get away!"

Praise God, I did not.

All the way through these last months of 2018 my friend Leslie had been walking with me even though she wasn't that far into her own journey of faith, maybe only two years. Anyway, she had started accompanying me to that church most Sundays leading up to the end of the year. Little by little it started to feel like a community for me, a community I could belong to, being part of smaller groups, serving the church in different ways. For the first time since I had played baseball, I felt that I was part of a team.

Church never felt like a difficult fit for me. I remembered how my older sister, Rosa, had tried to describe to me the reality of her conversion when I was six years old. Others might have said, "Oh, she's fallen in with a cult." But I never had a negative view about so-called "born-again Christians." At that age I didn't know her well. But she came across with such peace and serenity in her voice. She had self-control, and as I look back, it was evident that the Spirit of God was in her.

As the year rattled toward its conclusion, it was an extraordinary time. The same old familiarities of the approaching holidays, the lights decking out the city, the growing glow of Christmas drawing near, the streets and houses adorned with all kinds of seasonal decorations, the music, the movies. It's the same every year. It's easy to become inured to it all, right? But not this year. Not for me. This time it meant something different. The idea of advent — the coming of the King and the sense of expectation — carried a special promise for me this year. I couldn't put my finger on it exactly. But those old Christmas songs, the old motifs of a baby lying in a manger, of angels singing out over the world, "Peace and goodwill to all men" — they all seemed saturated with a new meaning to me. Joy was rising within me like a groundswell, surrounding me, overwhelming me.

Christmas Day came and went. And I still held that same joy within my heart — the joy of faith, of believing the truth of what it was all supposed to be about. I held it there delicately as a little bird cupped in my hands, gazing at it in wonder.

I was standing at a threshold. I sensed that. And the time had come to cross over.

It was December 31, 2018, the last day of a year that had unfolded like no other. Leslie and I were there in church and this time when the preacher invited anyone who was willing to lay down his or her life at Jesus's feet, I felt no resistance. I was ready to surrender, to give myself completely into the hands of the one who is joy.

And so, I prayed, *My life is no longer my own. I give it over to you, Jesus, my Lord and Savior. Jesus, you take the wheel of my life. Take me wherever you want me to go. I'm here to serve you. I surrender to you all that I am right now.*

I felt a sense of total acceptance, total forgiveness settle over me. And tears started to flow. What I was feeling wasn't overwhelming, and it wasn't emotionalism. It was a quiet resolution in my heart, a contract sealed, a covenant made. The tears were a mark of my sincerity in that moment.

Anyway, Leslie was there to console me, if *console* is the word. She was witness to my resolution. And I walked away from that place not anticipating that anything much would be different but at least sensing the resolve in my heart.

The Veil Falls

It wasn't until the next day, January 1, 2019, that the full measure of what had happened hit me. I was at the gym, as I often was in those days. It was busy. Everyone had his or her new year's resolutions to fulfil. The usual guys were around. I was among friends, all focused on their workouts. I was in front of a mirror doing bicep curls, going through the motions, while my thoughts were full of what had happened. I knew I needed to change, but somehow that change felt possible now. I didn't feel the creeping inertia of depression holding me back.

Music was filling my head, one of the worship songs they would sing at the church at the time: *I surrender. I surrender.* It felt like a song written for me for this moment. And as I watched the reflection of the weight move up and down, felt the pump in my biceps, tears started springing from my eyes.

And suddenly it was as though a dam had broken. The tears became a river, totally unstoppable.

I thought I was going nuts. I must be because I couldn't stop it. And yet I felt love. *Such love.* Love indescribable, love unending, a deluge of the purest love I had ever experienced, washing through me, undoing me.

I put the weight down and almost ran to the other side of the gym away from the gaze of these total strangers, fighting back the dam-burst of tears. I hurried to a bathroom stall and locked the door behind me, and there I sat for a while crying and crying, tears of . . . I don't know . . . tears of joy and sadness, tears of relief, tears of homecoming. And all the while I was feeling seen and fully known by that all-consuming love.

There I was, sitting on a toilet in a gym in Belleville, New Jersey, knowing with absolute certainty that there is a God and that He loves me, seeing at last that I had it wrong my whole life, that there *was* one who saw me, one who noticed me, and He had been watching over me my whole life. And now at last He was inviting me to go on to go a different way, to go His way.

The apostle Paul wrote in a letter to the church in Corinth, *Whenever someone turns to the Lord, the veil is taken away. For the Lord is the Spirit, and wherever the Spirit of the Lord is, there is freedom. So all of us who have had that veil removed can see and reflect the glory of the Lord* (2 Corinthians 3:16–18 NLT).

The veil had fallen for me.

I sat there for about forty-five minutes sobbing and sobbing as the music played in my ears until I was able to pick myself up and take myself out to my car. But there it continued. I sat in the car park for another hour, weeping and listening to music, praising God through lips wet with tears, thanking Him for His patience, for never abandoning me, for loving a wretch like me. I didn't deserve His love, I knew it. I was a sinner who had basked in the glory of the world. But now, at last, I was turned right side up, justified by the death of Christ Jesus.

"God, you exist," I kept murmuring. "I can't believe you exist . . ."

I see you, was the reply. *I've always seen you.*

I was baptized on January 24. I cried every day leading up to that event.

That day I was fully immersed in water, an outward sign of what was already true: that I had been fully immersed in the Spirit of God. The Spirit of God was in me and had been since I'd sat down on that toilet in a gym in Jersey.

I had started serving in Hillsong Church in New York City about a week before my baptism. It just felt like a completely natural thing to do.

Something else had happened, too. God had switched on my intellectual curiosity. I found myself drawn more and more deeply into reading the works of all kinds of Christian speakers and preachers, listening to endless talks and sermons online, especially so-called Christian apologists, a word that comes from the Greek legal word *apologia,* meaning a "reasoned defense." The whole discipline derives from a verse in the New Testament: *In your hearts honor Christ the Lord as holy, always being prepared to make a defense to anyone who asks you for a reason for the hope that is in you; yet do it with gentleness and respect* (1 Peter 3:15).

I was thirsty for wisdom, for knowledge about God and the Bible and the kingdom of heaven—what it all meant, how it all fit together (as if you could learn that in a short amount of time!). But I mention this as illustrative of the spiritual awakening going on in me. It was as if my mind were a house, and suddenly I had stumbled into a new room that I never knew was there before. I started taking ministry courses, one in my mother's area of the city, Cedar Grove.

It was at a church called Calvary Temple Church. I signed up for a pair of courses over two semesters called Elijah House Ministries that ran from February through May. Early on, perhaps in late January, I had a dream in which I saw myself standing in the dark. And then a spotlight turned on. In the brightness of the light I could just about make out that I was on a stage standing above an audience of people. But I couldn't see them well.

The light was too bright in my eyes. I didn't know what this meant exactly. It may have just been the product of an overactive imagination, or perhaps truly God was revealing more of me as He was revealing more of Himself. According to the Preacher in the book of Ecclesiastes, within the heart of every person God has planted a longing to know Him: *He has made everything beautiful for its own time. He has planted eternity in the human heart, but even so, people cannot see the whole scope of God's work from beginning to end* (Ecclesiastes 3:11 NLT).

Of course, we don't get to see the whole picture.

But as I listened to more teachers and pastors and then started going to these classes, I came to believe that God was calling me to preach the Word, not only to preach but also to tell, to proclaim the gospel of Jesus Christ, to tell people my story: what God had done for me and what He was beginning to do in me anew.

While I was coming to the end of the second of my two courses at Calvary Temple, I learned through Leslie that our own church, Hillsong, taught a more advanced series of courses at their theological center in Sydney, Australia, called Hillsong College. As soon as I heard about it, I had a longing to go there just to learn more about God. It was that simple.

But Sydney, Australia?

I mean, didn't they have somewhere a little closer? I had traveled to quite a few different places over the course of my life. But this was literally the other side of the world from New Jersey. But the burning impatience in me persisted. Once I got the idea in my head, I couldn't shake it.

I soon found out that you needed references to get accepted on any of their courses, and for that, you needed to have attended one of the accredited churches for at least six months. I hadn't even been a Christian for six months, let alone at a single church for that time. But I was so set on it that I applied anyway. The leadership at Hillsong in New York could see how determined I was and took pity on me; they signed off on a reference. Meanwhile at Elijah House Ministries it looked as though it would be a little harder. After all, they had known me only a few months there. But eventually I got a meeting with Reverend Dee, a lady who was the course facilitator over at Calvary Temple. She sat me down in her office and asked me to tell her my story.

An hour later, she had heard much of what you've read in these pages. When I stopped talking, she sat for a moment, thoughtfully tapping the surface of her desk.

"Tell you what I'll do," she said, suddenly all brisk and business-like. "I'm going to write you a reference right here and now. Can you wait?"

You bet I could!

I went out of that office clutching her letter as if I had just won the lottery. I packaged it all up with my application and sent it off to Australia in April. The afternoon I sent it off, I dropped Leslie off at her condo. She said she would pray for a positive answer.

"Wouldn't it be crazy if God gave me an answer on my birthday?" I joked. It was only a month away.

Maybe God thought that would be funny too. Because sure enough, on May 7, 2019, my fortieth birthday, I received an e-mail saying that I had been accepted into the July intake of the Hillsong College School of International Leadership.

Leslie and I had been hanging out a lot over the past seven months. There were moments when I thought I noticed a look from her, a look that said she might be harboring feelings that she wanted us to be more than friends. I eventually realized that maybe I hadn't been entirely fair with her. I had been leaning hard on her friendship. We had spent a lot of time together, journeying through this adventure of faith together. And from my side it never really occurred to me that we would be anything but friends. But one day I felt I ought to address this with her. It was an evening at Calvary Temple Church after a Wednesday night Bible study, and we had just finished class. As we moved outside with the others, I took her to one side.

"Leslie . . . I gotta ask you something — 'cause I want everything to be out in the open between us."

"Go ahead. What is it?"

"Do you have feelings for me?"

At first she said no. But that didn't feel like the end of it. Instead, I felt bold. I wanted to deal with this. Maybe that was the Holy Spirit working a change in me. But for once I didn't just want to slink away and pretend there was nothing that needed saying. I pressed her again. "Are you sure?"

Her eyes held mine, just for a second. "Look, I know that's not where this is headed. I mean, you're going to Australia, to Hillsong College. That's what you're doing. So . . ."

There wasn't much more to be said. My fear was that our friendship would cool off after that, that I had brought it to some kind of decision point and that if it wasn't going to progress toward more than it was, then we would inevitably drift apart. But I'm glad to say it didn't happen that way. We remained close friends. Whatever she would admit to, she understood that the next chapter for me would open on the other side of the planet.

Ultimately, though, we would lose touch once I had gone. Who knows if this was my fault? But I do know this: God places people in your life for a reason, sometimes for a season, sometimes for a lifetime. And I will always be grateful for Leslie's friendship during this extraordinary period of my life. She is truly one of God's vessels.

So, on July 24, 2019, I bid farewell to my mother, to Leslie, to my friends—and boarded Flight UA91 to Sydney, Australia.

Ten thousand miles and a world away.

CHAPTER NINE

His Image, Not Mine

When we begin to glimpse the reality of God, the natural reaction is to worship him. Not to have that reaction is a fairly sure sign that we haven't yet really understood who He is or what He's done.
- N.T. Wright

In the many hours I sat on the plane, flying west at thirty-five thousand feet above the Pacific Ocean, I had a chance to reflect on everything that had happened that had led me to that point, to this part of my journey.

And slowly I started recognizing not only my own part in the story but also the part of another actor, if you will, another person who little by little had been making Himself known to me, slowly stepping forward to take His rightful place front and center in my life.

Jesus Christ.

For a long time, I had pushed Him away and away until He was only the faintest whisper in my conscience, too easy for me to ignore, to drown out with other voices or to dull my hearing with alcohol or drugs or worse. But He never went away. He never left me. And slowly I began listening, slowly I began focusing, slowly I began surrendering to the truth and beauty and goodness of His words, of His presence and His Spirit.

He had begun placing people in my life, vessels of His grace and mercy, to protect me, to listen to me, ultimately to guide me back to Him: Marlon and Stephanie; Leslie leading me back to church; Jim, the leader of a small pastoral group at Hillsong who began guiding me in the faith and backing me when I was considering this move to Australia. Out of a room full of a hundred, I had felt drawn to him over all others when trying to figure how to connect with people in church. It was nothing more than a feeling at the time. But as I look back on it, it now felt like something ordained, something willed to happen. He heard my story, saw the passion in me, and knew what to do to connect me with the path forward.

And, of course, there had been Francisco that fateful night of the crash. If he hadn't stepped in at just the right moment and taken my keys off me, who knows if I would even be here?

So, this was how Jesus was coming into my life, through these people who knew Him, who responded to His promptings to carry out His will.

But more important than this, between those two important dates in my life — January 1 and January 24 (the date of my baptism) — I had felt the Spirit of God like the weight of glory on me. It was a feeling of saturation, of intimacy, like that of a newborn child being held in a mother's embrace. That was in essence the position I was in. But after the public declaration of faith at my baptism, that feeling had diminished, quietening into a steady reassurance of His presence, no longer the almost physical sensation that He was right there with me and in me. In fact, I missed that feeling. I would go to bed each night a little bereft, longing for that sense of the Father's embrace that had been so strong in those first days and weeks.

The apostle Paul talks about the fruits of the Spirit: "love, joy, peace, patience, kindness, goodness, faithfulness, gentleness, self-control" (Galatians 5:22–23). All of these felt so easy in those twenty-four days. Now — already — I had to grow up a little. I had to make choices. I had to move beyond naked emotion to my actual will to choose Jesus, to choose faith in Him, to choose to follow Him wherever He wanted to lead me.

I was learning that faith is not a subjective experience that fits around the narrative of your life. Rather, there's an objective truth to it, something outside yourself that you swing into line behind, a reality to which you submit. This was what I was learning I had to do.

A song titled *I Surrender* was significant at the time and would stir up deep emotions within me. The lyrics really spoke to me, expressing very accurately where I stood, what I wanted. Even now when I hear that song it triggers the memory of that deep longing within me, like a thirst in my soul that had always been there but only now was truly being acknowledged. Only now was at last being quenched.

Jesus said, "If anyone thirsts, let him come to me and drink" (John 7:37).

Well, I was thirsty. I had been for decades. By now I was desperate to drink from the true fountainhead. Only Jesus could satisfy that in me.

"Whoever believes in me, as the Scripture has said, 'Out of his heart will flow rivers of living water'" (John 7:38).

The joy that came with that surrender was like nothing else I had ever experienced in my life. It was unconditional love, divine love, a love that conquers all.

It certainly had conquered me and created in me a desire even now only to share that love with others, whoever will listen.

It's a two-pronged paradox. On the one hand is the hunger within us for self-will. We want to live our lives according to our own desires, our own needs, our own inclinations. We don't want some all-powerful God telling us what to do. We think Sinatra had it right: "I did it my way" because that must be the best way, the way to real freedom. But when we do, we instead find ourselves trapped in our own weakness, addiction, and folly. We become saturated with the consequences of our mistakes, we grow sick of heart and weary in spirit, until at last we are brought to our knees, begging God to reach down and help us — when really, He's always been right there, standing next to us, patiently waiting for us to hand Him the reins. And when we do, we discover the beauty of this mirror paradox: that in surrendering to Him, we gain the uttermost victory. In laying down our life to Him, suddenly we are born again. In dying to ourselves we are resurrected into a life of such vitality and fullness that we could never have imagined it. By submission we discover true freedom.

Truly . . . if that doesn't bring you joy, it's hard to know what will.

That is the good news. That is the gospel.

As I sat there on my flight to Australia reflecting on all of this, gazing out my little window at the stars that seemed so close in the dazzling heavens, I felt total peace that I was exactly where I needed to be. I didn't know what was going to happen to me next. My future was His. I had put it into His hands. But I felt safe in that uncertainty, sensing His light in that darkness.

From the New World to Down Under

As my plane touched down in Sydney, I had gone from the height of summer in New Jersey to the middle of an Australian winter. Even with the milder climate "down under," it was quite a drop in temperature. And I found the sudden switch of seasons immediately disorientating, not to mention the jet lag already starting to hit.

I won't deny that I was nervous. But they were good nerves. Folks back home in New Jersey had been blown away, not only by the mere fact that I would be taking myself off to Bible college. But Bible college in Australia? Many of my friends couldn't get their heads around that.

I had sold my share in the Krauzser's deli business back to my brother-in-law Darryl for a huge undercut. He thought I was crazy. He didn't want to hear anything about my reasons, didn't want to be "preached at," so he said. What I felt was faithfulness and determination, which he took for arrogance. How could I be so certain that I should dump my life in the United States to head off to Australia? That's the way he saw it. But in my mind, I was following where I felt God wanted me to go, so whatever the naysayers thought, I was confident He would find a way to work things out. (In fact, the money from that deal would pay fully for my three years of study, plus my housing during that time.)

So here I was on the far side of the world. Now what?

On the plane I had met another guy who was heading to Sydney to study at Hillsong College in the same program. We had boarded the same connecting flight in San Francisco and suffered the fifteen-hour flight together. He seemed to be one of those travelers who hated every minute of it, disgruntled, uncomfortable, disheveled. It was only when we landed, and he pulled on a Hillsong sweatshirt that I realized he was bound for the same destination as me.

His name was Heath. I quickly discovered that he was a musician from Colorado who was enrolled in what they called the "worship stream." Over the next year and a half, we shared together, we were to become good friends. The journey hadn't been kind to either of us; we felt rough as old boots. But once we had cleared customs, we were met by a welcoming party from Hillsong, ready to take us to our new home.

Naively, I had assumed that my accommodation for the year would be a modest apartment shared with perhaps one other person. In fact, on our arrival at our destination in a suburb called Glenwood, I discovered that we would be living in a five-bedroom communal household. At the age of forty, I admit it felt like quite a step backward in life. But it was even worse than I first thought — I had to share a bedroom too. Heath had been split off into other housing. So, I was dropped off at my new home with a younger guy named Danny, a thirty-one-year-old from Texas who was my new roommate.

Bumpy Landings

As I slung my bags down in our small room, rain was pelting down against the window. I was feeling wretched with jet lag, wanting only to crash on my own for a while, but that was not an option because, believe it or not, there were no beds yet. Another housemate named Chris told us that they were waiting for us in the garage. I look down at the old brown, damp-smelling, shaggy carpet that obviously had not been changed in decades. My roommate Danny was looking weary and bemused.

God, you've brought me here? Are you sure about this?

It was deflating. Perhaps I could be forgiven for a moment of doubt. It felt as though I had walked into a student dormitory. No, it is a student dormitory, I reminded myself. Reality and humility delivered a one-two smack in the face.

Danny and I exchanged glances. He shrugged and said, "Hey, man, it is what it is." He threw down his bag and said he was going to go find his bed. I wished I had his enthusiasm at this moment, or at least his resignation.

The beds turned out to be what even a ten-year-old would struggle to sleep in: tiny single beds that looked as if they had seen better days. Danny and I helped each other construct them. We were both so exhausted that once we were done, we threw ourselves down onto them with relish.

This is life now, I thought. And that's okay.

There was peace about everything I was doing. It was all humbling, for sure. But I didn't mind being humbled. And I had no doubts that I had done the right thing by leaving the United States to do this training here in Australia.

That night I discover the problem with Australian winters: the days are mild, but the nights are truly cold. Many Australian houses are built with no insulation. The first night was freezing cold. By the second, we had gotten ourselves a space heater from the local Kmart. I threw in an extra blanket and a new pillow for good measure. Even with this, we soon discovered that the heaters weren't up to the job. So those first couple of nights I slept in several layers of clothing, a hood pulled over my head. With the combination of the cold and the jet lag, I barely slept. These were without doubt two of the most depressing nights of my life. Danny took the whole experience better than I did. After all, he had lived in college accommodations before. I can't say I envy him.

On the positive side, Danny did prove to be a great roommate. He was easygoing and clean. Although a little quiet at first, he would soon warm up. Probably it was me who was the difficult one since I would often be up studying half the night.

But that would all come later.

Before the actual study, I first had to deal with the culture shock. Not only Australia and the surrounding suburbs of the city of Sydney (the area I lived in was called the "Hills") but also Hillsong Church itself, which took a lot of adjustment.

Australians abroad are famously laid-back, easygoing people. In their home environments they are perhaps even more so. Most of Sydney is a suburban sprawl. The central business district is small. It's the harbor that dominates the whole urban area, and the beaches, of which Bondi is undoubtedly the most famous. All this means that water and the ocean are a big part of the culture there.

Glenwood was a pleasant neighborhood, but sort of "vanilla." For me it didn't have a very strong flavor to it. It seemed a perfect place for young families, of which there were hundreds, a world away from the edginess of Newark, even though some "Hillsongers" would call it "Glen-hood" merely because there were a few incidents of theft. Mostly, though, everything from the housing to the parks to the shopping malls and restaurants and coffee bars was about convenience and recreation.

The Aussies are sports-mad, as we all know. And wherever you look there's someone exercising. Physically they are exceptionally beautiful people, I would say, maybe because they keep themselves so fit and healthy. Not long after arriving, I took a part-time job working in a chicken shop called Frangos. (One of my roommates had put in a good word for me with the manager, Carlos.) As I settled into the job, I would marvel how, observing the "true-blue" Aussies come and go in their natural environment, there seemed to be almost no ugly people among them. And they were all so polite. It was all "G'day, mate. How're you going?" making sure "everything's sweet with you" before they ordered what they wanted. Put simply, they had good manners, something you couldn't guarantee from the people where I came from.

These were my impressions anyway.

Despite all this, Hillsong Church had its own culture. It was a Christian bubble — which is an ambivalent statement. There were good things about that, but definitely bad things too. That said, I don't want to get distracted speaking negatively of Hillsong. They've had more than their share of detractors in the recent past. And after all, it was through them that I came to know Jesus as my Lord and Savior, so I owe them that.

Still, it's worth noting how what I saw and experienced at Hillsong impacted my own attitude and sense of where I was going.

Part of the clash came because I had gone there with a clear purpose in mind: I wanted to be trained as a pastor, whereas most of the young people attending the church seemed to want to be there only to belong to a big community. And Hillsong most definitely provided that: there were something like 1,600 students from over sixty nations at the college, and thousands more attending their Sunday services when I was there. I used to think of it as the Walmart of churches in Australia.

Of course, everyone is there ostensibly to worship God. But the subculture was all about meeting other young people; the music and the social scene were clearly also a big draw. For many, church became their tribe (their youth groups were literally dubbed "tribes"). That was sort of how it worked. Two of the pastors at the Hillsong church I had been attending in New York had warned me of this, or at least suggested I proceed with caution, that there was a risk of disappearing into the pleasant security of the Hillsong bubble and rarely coming out to experience the rest of the world.

It was too easy to stay wrapped up in the cocoon, they said. "Make sure you get out into the other churches and the other suburbs of the city." In any case, I was starting to realize that the people who needed reaching — those whom *I* wanted to reach anyway — clearly lived outside of that bubble too. So, I approached the entire culture of the church mindful of this phenomenon and went into it feeling the outsider very much.

At first, I was merely observing. Those I was sharing a house with came from different places around the world, and that was all good. The next group I met with was the pastoral leadership of the church. There was one leader, the first I would encounter who as head of the pastoral ministry of the church was responsible for processing the dozens and dozens of young people coming into the college. In a word, it felt like a factory conveyor belt. Here I was, fresh off the boat as it were, receiving my briefing. But it didn't feel personal in any way. I was just another number in that cohort.

I wasn't an actual person with a unique story. I suppose I didn't feel noticed again. And given how much I had cast aside to be there at the age of forty, that was disappointing to say the least. In fact, the guy was American, married to an Aussie. But it almost felt as though I was joining a firm rather than coming to be a disciple in a church, as if Hillsong were the JP Morgan of the Christian world, and the same spirit of excellence was what was expected of me, and I was expected to be impressed. Why? Well, because this was . . . Hillsong.

It's always dangerous when the brand becomes bigger than the mission.

Besides this, the questions he asked me felt not only very personal—why was I still single, aged forty? Was I in any significant relationship that they should know about? — but also as if he were ticking boxes to confirm that I fit certain criteria. It felt as if there were a template, and if you didn't fit it, then as an institution they didn't know what to do with you.

And it was clear from early on that I didn't fit their mold.

Part of the problem, I think, was that it was still a very short span of time since I had even come to faith, barely seven months. And in my enthusiasm to pursue full- time theological training as soon as possible, I was diving full-immersion into a very prescribed Christian culture. So, I hadn't made it easy for myself. But quite quickly I started questioning whether I even wanted to be a part of that church, let alone study full-time for three whole years in their college.

Nevertheless, however awkward the fit, I *was* learning things all the time, observing, processing, identifying things that I thought needed fixing, trying to make sense of what *I* could do to address the gap I perceived between seekers and believers. And as time unspooled, I started seeing myself standing as a bridge in that gap. I guess it was still so fresh in my head — what it felt like to be living in that "seeker" state of being in which you know something is wrong, you have a lot of questions and a sense that there *is* some answer that lies out there before you, but you just can't see what it is yet, only that the roads you have run down to find meaning in your life have all led to dead ends.

You feel that longing in your heart — for love, for value, for purpose.

As Jesus said, "Ask, and it *will* be given to you; seek, and you will find; knock, and it will be opened to you" (Matthew 7:7, emphasis added).

I had experienced the truth of those statements. And no matter the teething problems of fitting into a new culture, the bald reality that Jesus *is* the way, the truth, and the life was something I wanted to share with the world, with every person who was honestly seeking an answer, who was compelled to keep looking by his or her own sense of dislocation and frustration in life.

I still feel that compulsion, fueled by the love of God Himself, to reach out a hand to the lost. Because until so recently that was *my* hand too, groping in the dark. As it's often expressed, evangelism is just one beggar telling another beggar where to find bread. Well, I had found the Bread of Life, and above all I wanted to share Him with those who had not.

We must face facts. To outsiders, Christians often appear weird. And far too often Christians speak in a language that only highlights the distance between them and those who don't yet believe. It's off-putting. It's alienating. And ultimately it can cut people off from knowing the love of God.

All this said, there were individuals within the leadership with whom I found it easier to connect. The head of the master's program, Hadyn Nelson, was an exceptional pastor and academic for whom I still have endless respect. It was only because of him that I stayed with Hillsong College. By late 2019 and early 2020, just before the world melted down into the COVID-19 crisis, I was making serious plans to go on a mission trip to South Africa.

I had already started reaching out to pastors in that part of the world through the Hillsong global network. The only reason I didn't end up going was because I suddenly discovered I had a problem with my passport, which was about to expire and would take some time to fix. Then six weeks later the country was locked down, and no one was going anywhere.

I was bitterly disappointed. I had been desperate to get out into the mission field of South Africa. Instead, I was trapped along with everyone else in my home.

A New Creation

Meanwhile, I was not the same man I had been. Slowly the image of myself that over decades I had been building on false foundations was being slowly dismantled, and in its place something stronger, something truer was being revealed: God's own image of me . . . God's image *in* me.

Imago Dei.

You've read the account of my story this far. It's probably easy to identify that one of my biggest weaknesses was a desire to run after sexual relationships in an unhealthy way. I was looking for the answer to the question "Who am I?" in the women I was attracted to and wanted to be with. Even I could see that by now.

So, one of the changes that marked most clearly that something new was happening in me was that I felt no strong desire to get into a relationship — any kind of relationship — for about two years after my decision to follow the Lord. I went from being driven by a compulsive need to seek out the next sexual relationship and the next one — whether short- or long-lived — to feel good about myself, to finding a measure of peace in that area of my life. I stopped trying to fill that void in me with the approval and affirmation of a beautiful woman.

One example illustrative of this change was a date I went on in Sydney. The woman in question was a pretty blonde, very physically fit and perky, with a bubbly personality. In every way, she was the kind of woman I would have pursued in the past. It was a hot summer night late in January, and we were having dinner in an Italian bistro. To begin with, our conversation flowed nicely, along with the Moscato she was drinking. But when she asked me about myself, I started talking about Jesus. It felt like the only thing worth saying. I told her in not so many words that I believed Jesus is the only way to know God, that to have faith in Him is to have faith in the true and living God. After all, I explained, the story of my whole life at this point hinged on the life, death, and resurrection of Jesus Christ.

No doubt, you're probably thinking, *Way to kill the conversation, Michael!* And sure enough, across the table was a slight eye roll and a steadying sip on her glass of sweet wine. In the past I couldn't even imagine saying anything like this in a romantic context—but this was the new creation talking, the new Michael.

She composed herself. "How can you know all that for sure, Michael? I mean . . . I believe there are many ways that lead to heaven."

Notice how she reframed my claim?

It's the exclusivity of Jesus that often jars in conversations with strangers or, in this case, a pretty girl. Even though Jesus's arms were stretched wide on a cross, wide enough to include the whole world — in our culture the claim that *He* is the only way sticks in the craw. This is where boldness and courage are needed when defending the faith and being able to answer who God is, what He's done for us, what that means for the rest of the world. In a culture that holds "inclusivity" as the ultimate good, the "one way" of the gospel is hard to accept.

As our conversation continued, this girl went on laying out her syncretistic worldview, in which Buddha, Mohammed, and the gurus of the New Age all pointed equally valid ways to heaven. It was a view I had come across before, which unconsciously assumes a perspective that is superior to all other faiths and worldviews: from where it's possible to see that all of them lead to a good place, even though each of them is misguided in believing theirs is the only way. In other words, a view that claims to sit at the top of the mountain looking down on everyone else. It's a view that posits feelings as the ultimate guide, happiness as the goal, judgment as the ultimate sin, even while blind to the fact that it is judging its own conclusions superior to those of every other faith and belief system. In other words, the "all-inclusive" worldview is in the end as exclusive in its truth claims as all the rest.

Funny enough, the date ended a couple of hours later with little promise of another.

Afterwards we parted as friends, but slowly the friendship faded. I walked away from her, even though I knew the "old Michael" would have continued in pursuit, determined to win the approval and affirmation of such a beauty.

It wasn't as if I thought my understanding of God was better than hers or that I was somehow a better person. The reality was, I was a new creation, observing, processing and identifying who I would want to be with for the rest of my life who would run in parallel with me along this new road God was leading me down. At the end of the day, I wanted her to hear the gospel more than I wanted her to like me.

Noticing this change in me was another defining moment in my life.

It was a change that came not through anything I had done nor through some new discipline that I had found in myself. It just . . . happened. And I'm sure that was the work of the Holy Spirit in me, the gentle assurance from God that I was enough as I was, that I was valued as I was, that the answer to the question "Who am I?" was to be found in Him and nowhere else.

I didn't need to prove anything — to a girl like that, to Him, or to anyone else, and perhaps most importantly, to myself.

That was real freedom in an area that had caused me, and no doubt the women I had known, a lot of pain. I had a new heart now. And I didn't yet know where it would lead me.

There were, of course, still greater voids to fill in my heart, carved out by the absence of that father figure in my life. I don't know whether it was more painful through the years when my earthly father was "there but not there" for me, or else once he had passed on. I only know that after I lost him to cancer, Almighty God reached down from the heavens and little by little had supernaturally shown up in my life as my Father, my "Abba." As with the prodigal son of Jesus's parable, I had reached the end of myself. I was no longer chasing the world, popping pills and downing them with alcohol to dull the pain, no longer injecting steroids to impress or gain people's attention. What was the point of that, after all? To fill that unfillable void? It couldn't be done until at last it was my Heavenly Father who saw me stumbling toward him on the horizon and was filled with compassion. He ran to me, threw His arms around me, and kissed me. And in that reality, it was as if the thirst for my earthly father's approval was quenched once and for all. That void was filled to overflowing with the Father's love.

Chances are that many who are reading this book yearn for the love of their fathers as I did. Maybe that's you. If so, I implore you to call out to the Father, who dwells in heaven, who will never leave you or forsake you.

Pursue Him as though your life depends on it. Because it most certainly does.

Another change that came about in me was in confrontation.

I mentioned how I got a job working in a chicken shop called Frangos. I spent my days essentially serving people chicken burgers and half-chicken combos, which in the past I would have considered menial work, a role far beneath me. And yet I couldn't remember a time when I was so happy doing a job. It was basic stuff. I could have done it with my eyes shut. But I had such a spirit of peace and joy on me. I loved the little interactions with customers who would come to the restaurant, seeing them leave with their chicken and a little of the piece of the joy I was feeling, which I had given to them. The astonishing thing to me was how consistent this feeling was. Nothing could bother me, even though in objective terms it felt as if I had taken about five steps backwards in life. But that felt okay. And often I would wonder how on earth that was possible.

And believe me, this sense of peace was put to the test. The assistant manager of the shop was much younger than me, an Aussie born but of Middle Eastern ethnicity. He was a typical egotistical male, you could say, quite an unstable character whom we all knew was into taking a lot of drugs. Everything with him was about showing that *he* was the boss, that *he* called the shots. He used to take great pleasure, it seemed, in ordering me about, in yelling at me, belittling me, and generally being a pain in the neck. He did this to a lot of my coworkers as well.

The "old me" would have run out of patience almost immediately with this kind of behavior and told him off. But instead of feeling resentment and anger, I found myself praying for the guy. In my head, every day, I prayed for him! And even when everything came to a head and I had to address his attitude to me, it blew my mind how differently I handled that than I would have in the past.

One day he started yelling at me for supposedly cooking too many French fries. The whole staff in the place stopped what they were doing to watch the spectacle (they could hardly ignore it).

When he stopped to draw breath, I replied to him quite calmly, "Listen, man. Let's go outside and talk about this for a minute."

Now in most English-speaking countries an invitation like that means, "Outside now, 'cause I'm about to beat you into the ground." But instead, we went outside and genuinely I did just talk to the guy.

"Dude. What's going on? What's up with you?" "Nothing's up with me," he snapped defensively.

"Really? 'Cause you know you can't treat people like that. You should treat people with kindness and respect."

"What on earth are you talking about? I'll treat people how I like!"

"Listen. It's been two months that I've been putting up with this and I'm sorry, I can't work for you anymore."

I could hardly believe I was apologizing to him after he had belittled me in front of a dozen other staff members.

"Well, whatever, mate. It's no loss to us," was his sneery reply.

I nodded slowly, keeping my cool, then held out my hand. "Thanks for the opportunity anyway. Have a good one." Then I shook his hand and left.

It wasn't the end of it and I knew it wouldn't be. I knew I was doing the business a lot of good and that this guy had two other business owners senior to him who did rate what I was doing for them. One of them called me up and urged me to stay, promising I wouldn't have to work under that other guy anymore. In the end, I did stay for a little while longer, but I knew it was time to pivot. And before long I had found another job working in a gym right across from Frangos called Elite Fitness.

The whole episode seemed extraordinary to me. I knew the "old me" would have reacted in one of two ways: either (1) keep my head down and say nothing and take it or (2) blow up and get aggressive, up in the guy's face. (I admit there were times I wanted to choke the guy!) But this was new — this balance, confronting evil, if you like, or at least an obvious wrong, yet doing so with grace. And the result? It was grace that overcame.

To me this is part of the narrative we see in the Bible. After creation and the fall, redemption and restoration, comes the promise of the New Creation, starting with each person, one by one, coming willingly to be remade in Christ. This is not just another re-branding of an old model. This is literally a *new creation*, brought about not by my own hands nor by my own will but by the Spirit of God working in me, the same Spirit who will work in you, or anyone, if you choose to allow Him.

Paul wrote, *Your life is now hidden with Christ in God* (Colossians 3:3 NIV).

There is a mystery here: that the real you whom God intended to create is hidden in Jesus. The more you orientate your life around Him, the more you emulate Him, the more you will become the real you, the truest version of yourself—*His image in you.*

And finally, all of those false images we have tried to create for ourselves fall away from us.

Like the shedding of a serpent skin.

CHAPTER TEN

Image-Bearers, All of Us

There is no one who is insignificant in the purpose of God.
- Alistair Begg

I stayed at Hillsong College for a year and a half. This was only around half the length of time I had planned to study there.

During that time, and since, everything I've noticed, everything I've experienced has been shaping *how* I approach others with the good news of Jesus Christ. It's not enough to give answers to questions that a person isn't asking yet. It's not enough to make declamatory statements, however true they might be. You must meet the person where he or she is. And that means learning how to converse with someone in a way that opens first the person's ears and then the person's heart.

But it's been revelatory sharing my story through different encounters over the last three or four years. Often these encounters have resulted in responses that are quite different. But just as often, I've encountered responses that are effectively the same — similar barriers that people erect to keep them from knowing God in a personal and intimate way.

It started back in the United States with my friends and family.

The most common barrier took the form of relativity: "That sounds good for you, Mike. But it's not for me." And any perceived attempt to tell them otherwise is blocked out of hand. They're happy that you've found what they call "your truth" but won't entertain the idea that the same truth might apply to *them*, might demand anything of them.

I had this reaction countless times with friends in the United States when I was voicing my plans to go to Australia and why. I suppose it was a natural question for them to ask: "What's happened to Mike?" Sometimes the question was put in a sympathetic way, other times . . . not so much. But what was obvious to everyone was that *something had changed* in me, and that demanded some sort of explanation. The explanation they got, however, didn't always sit well with them.

After all, everyone — and I mean *everyone* — has a worldview (even if held unconsciously), a lens through which the person tries to make sense of the world. What I've noticed, however, is that very often people are not living in alignment with their own worldview. For example, an atheist worldview denies moral absolutes. It must. Because if atheism were true, there cannot be an absolute moral lawgiver, for such a being would be God. Thus, what an atheist considers is right or wrong, good or evil is no more than a matter of opinion, or worse a matter of taste. Put another way, what someone believes to be right or wrong carries no more philosophical weight than whether a person likes chocolate-flavored ice cream or vanilla. But when someone sleeps with his wife, steals his car, or abuses his children, the last thing you'll hear an atheist say is: "Well, it's just my opinion, but I believe that was wrong." Of course, they scream with moral outrage as loudly as the rest of us, and rightly so.

These days especially, everyone is screaming that one thing, or another is evil, that one group of people or another is evil, even if they don't agree on where that line should be drawn. Many of these same people also try holding on to the belief that there is no God. But those two positions are in direct contradiction. Therefore, one of them (or both) must be false. So, the atheist finds himself or herself either having to deny the existence of evil (hard to do in the face of human experience), or else the atheist must deny his or her philosophical position that God does not exist. The atheist can't have it both ways. Yet many try doing just that. That's what I mean when I say people don't live by their worldview. Or as the apostle Paul put it, there are people who "by their unrighteousness suppress the truth" (Romans 1:18).

The truth is suppressed, not denied.

This is what I've discovered and witnessed many times: the suppression of truth. But the truth cannot be suppressed forever. Jesus identified Himself as "the truth" (John 14:6). They nailed him to a cross, stabbed him with a spear, and slung his body into a grave. And yet *still* He came back. The truth always does. You might hide it, twist it, obscure it. But it cannot be destroyed.

So, when I would explain to people what had happened to me, most would hear me out. But again, they would gloss over what I had said. And this even happened with close family. It still does today to some extent. Blame easy cultural slogans or characterizations; blame the latest memes on TikTok or Twitter. But it always boils down to the same thing: denial. Because when a person is converted to a belief in Jesus Christ and that is evident in his or her life, when a person is born again in the Spirit, it is a challenge to people's reality. Either they must look at me and conclude that I've lost my mind or that I've been deluded into believing the lie of some religious cult—or else it must be genuine. But mostly people turn and run from the dilemma, screened behind comments like: "That's great. I'm happy for you."

But that's exactly what I want to be now — the irritant, the stone in someone's shoe, the little nagging doubt that maybe reality isn't exactly as they've neatly packaged it up to be or how they would like it to be.

It was hard in that respect, those first weeks and months. As the one experiencing the seismic changes in my life, there were times when even I asked myself, *Am I losing my mind?* I felt and acted like a completely different person. What on earth could bring that about? In those early days I lacked the confidence and boldness to fully explain the Christian faith, or even the gospel (probably my understanding of it was inadequate anyway). All I could say was what had happened to me. I could tell my story. And that's what I did.

Before I flew to Australia, for those first months of 2019 my mother would often listen to me talking as I sat at her kitchen table. "Where is my son?" she would ask, half loving, half mystified. I would sit and talk and often there was a newfound depth to what I was saying and the way I was now seeing the world. It was wisdom but it wasn't necessarily *my* wisdom, as if I had suddenly become wise. It was the Spirit of God within me leading me into wisdom, just as he promises.

"¿Dónde está mi hijo?"

Where is my son?

In some ways, she was on to something. The old Mikey had died. And I didn't yet know who this new Michael Cabezas would be.

In these new and uncharted waters, there was one shining star who gave me some reassurance. That was my sister Rosa.

Rosa was the sister who had come to faith when she was twenty. She was the one who had set me down as a six-year-old next to her, feet dangling once again but not in a church pew, rather on the couch in the family living room. There she had tried to explain what it was that she had discovered.

This time it was me telling her my story over the phone (She lives in Pennsylvania, so I didn't see her in person very often).

"So, I hear you're planning to move to Australia," she said matter-of-factly.

"That's right."

"Wanna tell me what's going on, Michael?"

"Sure." So, I did — the broad strokes of it anyway. I didn't need her to hear every detail. But I did tell her that I had gone through a radical conversion of faith. "I now sense God is real, Rosa . . . that He's revealed Himself to me," I said, trying to articulate the ineffable. "I feel . . . I feel His love all around me. It's undeniable."

For a moment there was silence on the other end of the phone. I started filling it with further explanations but then she just stopped me. "You don't need to say any more, Michael. I know exactly what you've been through. It was the same for me . . ." Then, "Welcome to the kingdom, little brother."

I can still hear those words to this day.

I felt my heart awash with relief. "I don't know, Rosa. Sometimes I feel like . . . like I'm going crazy. It's all so different. So new and unknown."

"You're not going crazy, Michael. I've met with Him too. That's what I tried to tell you back when it happened to me." "I know . . . I know." For a fleeting moment I almost wished I could be six years old again, attending to her words with greater care, hearing her and understanding better the path she was trying to show me, even at that tender age. "You feel different because you *are* a different person now,

Michael," she said gently. "You're a child of God."

Rosa had been much bolder than I was when she came to faith. I think she had rubbed many members of my family the wrong way. It had left a bitter aftertaste to anything to do with "too much" talk about Jesus. But my mother had to process not just one child coming to a deeper faith in Him — remember that we were all nominal Catholics already — but now a second child. This had a profound impact on her. She was often on the phone to Rosa asking about me, trying to find out more, to make sense of how different I was. And I think in time she came to accept the reality of it.

You might accept the testimony of one witness if you really trust that person, but often people do not. But the testimony of the two, in very different ways but pointing at the same truth? For my mother, eventually the evidence of her own children's lives was compelling. She has since committed her life to Jesus as her Lord and Savior and has been baptized anew. It's been a happy ending for Mom.

There have been other encounters with people not so close to me that illustrate the several ways in which people in this time and this culture are blinded to the truth.

A couple of months after I had started working at Frangos in Bella Vista, one of the managers came in and sat down with me over lunch one day.

"So . . . how d'you end up in 'Straya, mate?" he asked. "What do you mean?"

"You're forty, aren'tcha? Must have a bit of a back story. So, let's hear it."

Over the next five minutes or so I gave him my testimony, that I was here to pursue what I believed was a calling on my life. He gave me what I now knew was a typical response: "I'm happy for you, mate. Sounds like you've found what you were looking for." Even though I had heard this many times before, this time especially there seemed to be a kind of envy behind his words, as if what he meant to say was: "I want that too." But he held his poker face, even though he knew he held no cards and wanted to fold. Pride wouldn't let him.

When I tried explaining that it wasn't just "for me" — that the same promises of Jesus, the same rewards of salvation and knowing God awaited him as they had me — the mood between us cooled considerably. He became defensive, saying that he was a Catholic, at least by association, even though he wasn't practicing. He said he did "good things" and attended church on holidays. He even wore a crucifix around his neck as if these things would qualify a person to enter heaven. What more was there to faith?

But he couldn't bear the thought of one minute's conversation about the figure whom he literally carried around with him every day around his neck. He was dismissive of the whole notion that the love of Jesus might have significance for him personally. Even more so that this might lead to some necessary changes in his life or that such changes might even be for the better. It was eye-opening to me — the sincerity with which someone might applaud the good thing that happened in my life, but the moment there's any suggestion that this might point to something true about reality that demands a response from the person . . . shut down. The door slams closed.

Such is the cold fact of our own self-will. We want to live our lives exactly as we decide. We don't want to change, certainly not on the strength of someone else's experience. After all, I was the same. I had heard of my sister's experience when I was six. It was another thirty years before my ears were ready to truly hear the message of the gospel.

As Jesus said, *He who has ears to hear, let him hear* (Matthew 11:15).

I did afterwards wonder whether I could have approached the conversation in a better way. No doubt I could have. But it was suddenly very clear to me that most people don't follow through on what they believe. In other words, they don't know who they are, what they believe, what their purpose is, and what that means for the rest of the world. As it's often said, if you don't stand for something, you'll fall for anything.

Imago Dei

I started to realize that maybe what people needed to hear was the very basic message that every person who exists and ever existed is made in the image of God. We, you, are the *imago dei*. Every one of us is an image-bearer of our creator. That fixes us within certain parameters of existence — of value, identity, purpose, ultimate meaning, good and evil, the unfolding story of our lives. We aren't just a cosmic accident trying to stitch together a few experiences into a patchwork life that we might call happy or fulfilling.

There is a call on each of our lives. God intended us, made us for a purpose, and is calling us into that purpose at every single moment of our existence — because He loves us with such abandon that He was willing to die for us, even after we had rejected Him, turned from Him, and gone our own way. He is eternally ready to welcome us back if only we would turn . . .

So much pain exists in the world because we have forgotten this basic underlying fact of our existence. We live our lives like orphans, fending for ourselves, exploiting and manipulating each other for our own gain because we think there's no other way to meet our needs. We have forgotten that there is a father who rules over all, who loves us and to whom we owe every breath we take.

God reigns. God satisfies. This is what He promises through the life, death, and resurrection of His Son, Jesus Christ, a promise He will never break. Every one of us owes Him everything, literally everything. And yet like spoiled kids we've turned away, we've gone chasing after other idols, making gods of things that cannot satisfy, pouring out our lives in worship to things that are bound to break our hearts. And we go on and on doing so until we can take no more. Only then might we be ready to hear the whisper that has always been on our shoulders: *Come home. Come home, my child . . .*

And when we do, we do not receive the chastisement we deserve. Instead, we're welcomed with open arms. Love, love, love envelopes us, sweeps us up into a new story, the story we were meant to follow all along. We are redeemed, rescued, restored. We are healed of all our wounds. And what's more, we are elevated to the fullness of the life that God always wanted for us from the beginning.

New creations in Him, for Him, and by Him.

To God be the glory forever and always.

Amen.

Epilogue

*The wind blows where it wishes, and you hear its sound, but you do
not know where it comes from or goes. So, it is with everyone who is
born of the Spirit. (John 3:8)*

As I sit on an outdated beach chair on the island of Bohol,
Philippines, it is the first day of November 2023. The sun
blazes through the palm trees, and I have one thought:
Thank you, God. I can't help but be grateful. The wind
suddenly picks up and embraces me.

There you are, Father.

The wind blows, but my will stays firmly anchored in
our cornerstone, Jesus Christ. So much has happened since
my time with Hillsong College and then Alphacrucis
University. I've recently obtained my certification in
apologetics from Biola University, and I plan on completing
postgraduate work in counseling in 2025. I've also been
quite the traveler this year — from Colombia to Scotland,
England to New York, and Sydney to the Philippines.

I venture on with my ministry, traveling wherever I go,
asking people what they believe, why they believe it, and
what that means for the rest of the world. I do this by first
offering people a semi-professional photograph of
themselves which I then take, of course. My new Canon
camera has been the best sidekick a guy looking to

evangelize could ever have! This is a form of what philosopher Francis Shaffer would call "pre-evangelism" — opening a conversation, opening up a person's ears.

He who has ears to hear . . . right?

I don't always get to communicate the gospel in all its fullness. But I plant some seeds and leave them for others to water, so to speak. As Christian apologist and author Greg Koukl says, "Some are meant to be gardeners and some harvesters." I'm okay with being the former.

I also refer them to my website for more information on who I am and how they can find me.

As I leave you, I would like to focus on John 3:8 (the verse opening this epilogue) and its overarching meaning for you and me. You cannot see the wind, but you know the wind is there because there is sound, pressure against your skin, or branches and leaves and sand caught up in the air. As pastor and theologian John Piper reminds us, "The movement of the Spirit does not originate with *us*; we don't control His direction. Furthermore, we can't determine His origin or His destination. The Spirit is free. He goes where He wills."

The Spirit's will, moreover, *is* decisive. To be sure, our own will moves in the moment of new birth. Change happens in us. Ours wills are awakened and moved toward Christ because the Spirit blows where He wills and gives life to *whom* He wills. This is what it means to be "born again". That event is decisively and ultimately the work of the Spirit's will, while secondarily and dependently the act of our will. God patiently awaits our *yes* and *amen* — two wills then, which result in a new creation.

Today, dear reader, are you seeking out things from the world that are empty and unfulfilling? Are you going through something that's eating you up inside and you just can't let go? Are you looking for peace, love, and joy that transcends time, space, and matter? Perhaps the wind of the Spirit is blowing through your heart this day.

If so, then I urge you to do as Jesus commands, to be born again:

Truly, truly, I say to you, unless one is born again he cannot see the kingdom of God (John 3:3).

I hope and pray to see you there.

About the Author

Michael Cabezas never imagined writing his radical testimony on paper for the world to read. But God had other plans for him. Now, five years later, that time has come and in the words of G.K. Chesterton, "One of the most necessary and most neglected points about the  story called history is the fact that the story is not yet finished."

Similarly, Michael hopes his testimony will live on through readers by seeking purpose, meaning, and value through the teachings of Jesus Christ. He prays that readers have been inspired, encouraged and that his memoir will serve as a beacon of light for those navigating their spiritual journey, guiding them toward a deeper relationship with the one source of hope and salvation.

Michael currently lives in Sydney, Australia, enjoys munching on soft, chewy chocolate chip cookies, embraces singlehood, and is an avid reader of Christian apologetics and counselling theories. He holds a bachelor's in business administration/theology and certificate of apologetics from Biola University.

For more information, or to get in touch, please visit www.MichaelCabezas.com

www.ingramcontent.com/pod-product-compliance
Lightning Source LLC
Chambersburg PA
CBHW021446150726
47989CB00001B/415